SHIPS AND MEN OF THE GREAT LAKES

Also by Dwight Boyer

STRANGE ADVENTURES OF THE GREAT LAKES

TRUE TALES OF THE GREAT LAKES

GHOST SHIPS OF THE GREAT LAKES

GREAT STORIES OF THE GREAT LAKES

SHIPS AND MEN
OF THE
GREAT LAKES

by Dwight Boyer

Illustrated with photographs and maps

DODD, MEAD & COMPANY
NEW YORK

1 2 3 4 5 6 7 8 9 10

Library of Congress Cataloging in Publication Data

Boyer, Dwight.
    Ships and men of the Great Lakes.

    Includes index.
    1. Shipwrecks—Great Lakes. 2. Great Lakes—History.
I. Title.
F551.B718   977'.03   77–5901
ISBN 0–396–07446–4

Acknowledgments

In a retrospective assessment of the trials and travails involved in writing a book of this nature, one is acutely conscious of the host of friends and Great Lakes buffs who have contributed greatly, not only in data and material, but in time and encouragement.

There comes immediately to mind Janet Coe Sanborn, the respected and astute editor of the Great Lakes Historical Society's quarterly, *Inland Seas*, and other Society stalwarts, the Reverend Alexander C. Meakin, Andrew Sykora, Howard Baxter, Dan S. Connelly, Roman Keenan, William D. Carle III, and Lawrence A. Pomeroy, Jr.

And I was constantly amazed at the dedication of librarians who, when given scant clues and sketchy information, responded with the enthusiasm of true historians. I refer to people such as Mrs. Ruth Revels of the Milwaukee Public Library, Mrs. Janet Bean of the Chicago Public Library, Mrs. Mary C. Lethbridge of the Library of Congress, Nicholas N. Smith of the Ogdensburg, New York, Public Library, and Mrs. C. B. Andrews of the Erie County Historical Society, Erie, Pennsylvania.

Then, too, there were others who willingly spent many hours in research on my behalf. Among them were John A. Chisholm of Muskegon, Michigan, Ken LaFayette of Marquette, Michigan, and Edward N. Middleton of Kansas City, Missouri, a gentleman whose enthusiasm in researching Lake Michigan material knows no bounds.

There were many others, of course, including Milton J. Brown, Captain John A. Mitchell, Bruce W. Hedderson, George Egbert, Jackie Keough, Paul Kissman, George Womer, Stephen A. Blossom, Mrs. Merle Gerred, George A. Vargo, Captain George Hanson, Al McGinty, James E. Eagles, Dr. Julius F. Wolff, Jr., Frank Dadante, Merle George, Robert I. Schellig, Jr., Captain John Leonard, Robert Skuggen, Margaret M. Jacobs, Adolph Anderson, Richard V. Cordo, George E. Condon, Dick Burke, Walter and Teddy Remick, Robert Scott, Don Williams, Irene Waisanen, Charles Meadows, Earl Gagnon, John Huth, Peggy Scruton, Verna Gamble, Richard Wager, Chandler Harris, Earl C. Hartson, Captain Frank J. Gerkowski, William L. Kaiser, Duff Brace, Merl Gibbon, Thomas O. Murphy, Captain Edgar M. Jacobsen, Elwyn E. Wilson, Captain Norbert Fahey, and Robert E. Lee of the Dossin Marine Museum in Detroit. Special help, too, came when it was most needed, from Thomas O. Murphy of Cleveland, and W.A.W. Catinus, Chief of Marine Casualty Investigation, Department of Transport, Canada.

Men of the United States Coast Guard have also been helpful, among them Rear Admiral James S. Gracey, commander of the Ninth Coast Guard District, Lieutenant Commander Arthur Whiting, Captain James A. Wilson, and Lieutenant Dan Shotwell.

My associates at the *Plain Dealer*—Dolores Fischer, James A. Ross, James F. Gayle, Andrew Cifranic, Ralph J. Meyers, Richard B. Kendzierski, Dick Dugan, Nickolas Dankovich, and Vincent Matteucci—were also extremely helpful.

Then too, long talks with Dennis N. Hale, the sole survivor, were helpful in documenting the last hours of the *Daniel J. Morrell* and her people.

And, of course, a special note of gratitude is due my wife, Virginia, whose critical eye caught many a redundancy and misplaced comma.

DEDICATION

For well over a century ships and men of the Great Lakes have vanished from the face of the earth. Old-timers used to say that they just "sailed through a crack in the lake." But there are no cracks in the lakes—just great, roaring storms, lurking shoals, and all the hazards faced by sailors since the day when man first went down to the sea in ships.

Most of the missing are from another era, before the present aids to navigation were conceived or dreamed possible. But modern man with his ingenious devices and technological advances is still humbled by the great forces of nature and unseen adversaries.

What better example can be offered than the fate of the big steamer *Edmund Fitzgerald?* She disappeared in Lake Superior on the terrible night of November 10, 1975, apparently only moments after her skipper reported by radio to another vessel, "I am holding my own. We are going along like an old shoe. No problems at all."

So, sadly, to my good friend John H. McCarthy, her first mate, and the other gallant men of the "Fitz," this book is respectfully dedicated.

Captain	Ernest M. McSorley
First Mate	John H. McCarthy
Second Mate	James Pratt
Third Mate	Michael E. Armagost
Wheelsman	John D. Simmons
Wheelsman	Eugene W. O'Brien
Wheelsman	John J. Poviach
AB Maintenance Man	Thomas D. Borgeson
Watchman	Ransom E. Cundy
Watchman	William J. Spengler
Watchman	Karl A. Peckol
Maintenance Man	Mark A. Thomas
Maintenance Man	Paul M. Riippa
Maintenance Man	Bruce L. Hudson
Deck Cadet	David E. Weiss
Steward	Robert C. Rafferty
Second Cook	Allan G. Kalmon
Porter	Frederick J. Beetcher
Porter	Nolan F. Church
Chief Engineer	George J. Holl
First Assistant	Edward Bindon
Second Assistant	Thomas E. Edwards
Second Assistant	Russell Haskell
Third Assistant	Oliver Champeau
Oiler	Blaine H. Wilhelm
Oiler	Ralph G. Walton
Oiler	Thomas Bentsen
Special Maintenance	Joseph W. Mazes
Wiper	Gordon MacLellan

Contents

SHIPS AND MEN OF THE GREAT LAKES

1

⚓

Ach! Wer Ist John Maynard?

Wer ist John Maynard?

Yes, indeed, where is John Maynard?

It is a valid, perplexing question simply because the mortal and humble wheelsman who sacrificed his own life to save others never answered to that name in real life. Though he became eulogized in prose, poem, and sermon in many languages, thus achieving timeless stature in literature, there never really was a John Maynard.

His name was Augustus Fuller, although here again some who have chronicled his noble deed have been led to believe that his given name was Luther. Not so. However, none would take issue with the documented fact that he was, as his captain later stated, "a resolute man."

As it transpired, he was far more resolute than the captain.

Augustus Fuller was one of three wheelsmen aboard when the big wooden sidewheeler *Erie* departed her dock at Buffalo at 4:10 on the afternoon of August 9, 1841. He

1

shared bunk space with Jerome McBride and James Lafferty, the other two wheelsmen.

The *Erie* was a rather large and commodious vessel for her time and required a considerable crew, including four cooks, assorted porters, and waiters and maids, all under head steward Leander Jolls. There were also two barbers and a passable ship's band comprised of crew members with a musical bent. The latter all had more important shipboard duties but met briefly for departure fanfares and unusual occasions.

The *Erie* was typical of many steamers serving the freight and flourishing immigrant and domestic passenger trade out of Buffalo, with stops at Erie, Cleveland, Detroit, and Chicago. It had a typical passenger list, too. In addition to the usual commercial travelers, several New York State families were moving to the territories of Michigan, Wisconsin, and Minnesota, bringing aboard their total possessions. So were a large number of immigrants, all seeking to begin new lives in the promised land. Several nationalities were represented, but the roster was heavily Swiss— over one hundred out of a full passenger manifest of three hundred. The Swiss passengers, having traveled as a group from their homeland, had been booked for the voyage by Messrs. P. L. Parson & Company, agents, of Buffalo.

The departure was a familiar sight for those working on the docks. Buffalo was the small end of the funnel for hopeful immigrants who arrived from the east by canal boat and continued their westward journeys on lake vessels. No other mode of transportation was available for people traveling with their worldly possessions, to say nothing of numerous children. The George Nelgold family, for example, totalled eight. Broods of six and seven were common. A peculiarity inherent in the immigrant trade, was that the heads of the households were burdened night and day with carpetbags. In every case they contained the family's cash reserves, which would finance the beginnings of a new era in a strange world. It was common knowledge that one of the Swiss gentlemen, John Voegele, was accompanied by 25,000 florins in addition to his wife and nine children.[1] Unlike many of the passengers, most of the Swiss were destined for Ohio, where previous friends and relatives in Cleveland, Akron, Dover, Zanesville, Portsmouth, and Massillon had already arranged accommodations.

Who knows what ambitions, missions, errands, or business details occupied the minds of the other passengers? In any mixed group thrown together for a voyage, friends are quickly made and seemingly incongruous stories and rumors are rampant. Some curiosity had been aroused when a sleek and sometimes skittish horse had been led aboard. It was later explained that it was a race horse owned by one of the passengers, a Mr. Carpenter. More prosaic was the case of Valentine Ackerman, a tinner, who was merely going as far as Erie to visit his parents.[2]

Of more importance, since their presence literally deter-

[1] Years after the *Erie* burned to her water line and sank, a crew of itinerant, free-lance salvagers raised the charred hull and towed it to Canada. There, carefully sifting through the grisly debris, they found what they suspected would be there—the hard cash with which the immigrants had hoped to establish themselves in America. They found it melted into lumps that were still highly negotiable for the gold content.

[2] Valentine Ackerman had been working in Buffalo and was en route to visit his parents, near Erie. Valentine, Sr., and his wife, Susan, lived on a nineteen-acre farm south of the community, a plot that is now well within the city limits.

mined the subsequent fate of all the others, was the em-
barking of William G. Miller of Buffalo, accompanied by
Messrs. Sears, Barbier, Weaver, Thomas, Evarts, and Fin-
ney, painters in his employ. They were en route to Erie,
where Mr. Miller had contracted to paint and redecorate
the steamer *James Madison*. But of even more importance
was what they brought with them—cans of paint, brushes,
and turpentine.

In the usual bustle and confusion that marks the beginning of a voyage, when the luggage and property of passengers departing at the first port of call are logically placed
where they will be easily accessible, the painters placed
their demijohns of turpentine on a ledge on the main deck.
Unthinkingly, they selected a point directly over the
boilers.

With the *Erie* outward bound and the sun still very
bright, Captain T. J. Titus made his routine log entries
and prepared for dinner.

Historians have often fantasized about the scenes aboard
the *Erie* in the early hours of the voyage, envisioning the
promenade deck crowded with starry-eyed immigrants and
happy children at play. Actually, a brisk wind had been
blowing all day, developing a distinctly rough sea. The
Erie rolled and pitched unpleasantly. Instead of enjoying
a bountiful dinner, as the historians have assumed, nearly
every child and most of the women were in their bunks,
dreadfully seasick, as were many of the men. Nor, as has
been written, was the night inky black when the inevitable
happened.

The sun, on August 9, set at 7:57 P.M., and a lingering
twilight with excellent visibility persisted for some time.

The *Erie* was off Silver Creek, New York, Captain Titus was in the pilot house, and Augustus Fuller was at the wheel when, at eight o'clock, the demijohns of turpentine, carelessly placed on the overhead above the boilers, exploded.

Instantly everything in the vicinity was ablaze. Then the cans of paint blew up, showering their flaming contents over much of the midship area. Flaming turpentine and paint rained down into the boiler room and fire hold. In just a few seconds the flames burst through the skylights, towering above the topsided framework of the walking-beam engine. Driven by brisk winds, the flames swept aft with frightening speed.

Panic-stricken immigrants and other passengers, given little choice by the mushrooming inferno amidships, rushed either to the bow or stern. The staterooms and cabins were already being consumed with a fire of such intensity that there was simply no opportunity for escape.

Thirty-three-year-old Captain Titus was a realist. The wooden-hulled passenger vessels of the day were exceedingly vulnerable to fire. Several had already taken substantial tolls in human life. He had experienced no such problems with his previous steamboat commands, the *Ohio* and *Sandusky*, but now it was apparent that fate had chosen him for a principal role in what was undoubtedly shaping up as one of the great tragedies of the century. The explosion and frightful scope of the resultant fire left no doubt as to the only logical decision he could make.

Grabbing helmsman Augustus Fuller by the shoulder, he ordered him to swing the vessel hard aport and head for shore, still clearly discernable as a long, blue, and seemingly endless prospect of land. Fuller immediately hauled the *Erie* around on her emergency course, although even then the flames were sweeping speedily and relentlessly toward his station in the pilot house.

"Stick it out as long as you can," Captain Titus ordered before departing on urgent business elsewhere. The urgent business, succeeding generations of sailors and historians suspect, was that of saving his own hide.[3]

Once the course was changed, the *Erie* fell into the trough of the seas and rolled heavily. She was no longer heading into the wind and the fire, instead of being driven aft, now swept with measured rapidity in both directions. Above the roar and crackling of the fire could be heard loud reports as superheated iron bolts and stays gave way.

The pace of the steamer gradually slowed as the steam pressure dropped. Some of the firemen and engineers had been incinerated almost immediately. Others, although badly burned, escaped. Obviously there came a time when, the steam pressure gone, the *Erie*'s laboring sidewheels slowed to a crawl and finally stopped. Still rolling, she lay there in the troughs of the seas, a helpless pyre.

From the moment of the explosion and vomiting of flaming turpentine and paint, there had been frenzied attempts of passengers to throw overboard anything that would support human weight. Chairs, benches, tables, boxes, and

3 Great disasters of the era were frequently depicted by artists and these lithographic reproductions, however imaginative or fanciful, were widely distributed. The lithograph produced by the Buffalo firm of Hall & Mooney has Captain Titus standing calmly at a gangway opening immediately aft of the sidewheels, although this could hardly be possible. About twenty-five people, pursued by flames, are clustered at the bow; others are shown jumping or already in the water. Our hero wheelsman, whom the artist's legend identifies as Luther Fuller, is portrayed still at his post, nearly surrounded by flame and smoke.

baggage went tumbling overboard. Ropes that held the ship's fenders were slashed free, followed instantly by fear-crazed passengers and crew seeking refuge on the heavy wooden fenders. A few managed to reach some objects to sustain them. Others disappeared almost at once in the choppy seas that came over them with relentless frequency. A cabinet that supposedly held life preservers, located near the source of the fire, was immediately inaccessible and quickly destroyed.

The entire after end of the vessel was now in flames. A few souls who had stuck it out were hanging from the severed fender ropes, the rudder, and sidewheel frame-work. But when the searching flames found them, they, too, plopped off into the seas to disappear.

Among the few to escape was Captain Titus. He had, through his intimate knowledge of the vessel, found his way to the spot where his yawl boat was lashed. Others among the frenzied passengers and crew had already found and launched the yawl only to have it swamped repeatedly by overloading and their inability to manage it. He jumped into the sea and managed to get a grip on the capsized craft's keel.

Meanwhile, what of gallant Augustus Fuller? The pilot house was practically untenable within a few moments after the explosion and rapid spread of the fire. Still he hung on, although the smoke and flare of flame made the *Erie's* compass somewhat of a mockery. Flames now shot up from below and licked furiously all around him. Still he clung to his post, even when the distant blue horizon could no longer be seen. Finally the pilot house super-structure collapsed and plunged down through the main deck into a jumble of flaming and crackling beams and ship's gear. Augustus Fuller had paid the highest price a mortal soul can offer to his fellow men.

Two hours after the fire began, the steamer *Dewitt Clinton*, attracted by the glow on the horizon, hove to on the scene and began to pick up the scant few left of the *Erie*'s crew and complement of passengers. Altogether, the number saved, including a few rescued by small boats that had put out from shore, numbered less than fifty. Significantly, the list included Captain Titus and Augustus Fuller's two fellow wheelsmen, Jerome McBride and James Lafferty.

A coroner's jury inquiry, promptly impaneled, developed testimony diametrically opposed to the conditions as espoused by subsequent chroniclers of the *Erie*'s last voyage. It had still been light, not inky black, when the demijohns of turpentine exploded. Furthermore, a rough sea had prevailed from the moment of departure from Buffalo. This being the case, the women and children, instead of gamboling on the promenade deck, had mostly been below in the bunks, very seasick. This became more apparent when it was noted that of the more than one hundred children aboard, not a single one had survived, trapped, no doubt, by the inferno of burning turpentine and paint. Enforcing this grim conclusion was the fact that of the many wives and mothers aboard, only one woman, Mrs. Charles Lynde, survived. She was rescued by the *Dewitt Clinton*, along with Theodore Sears, one of the painters whose thoughtlessness had triggered the holocaust.

It was at the inquest that Captain Titus, referring to his heroic wheelsman, Augustus Fuller, said piously, "He was always a resolute man!"

In marine circles the frightful ordeal of the *Erie* and her people was subject to much gossip and debate. But there was a philosophic vein to all discussions. It was a point of fact that all such vessels were almost identical in construction and therefore prey to identical disasters. One could only hope that better supervision and inspection of cargoes and baggage accepted would preclude such idiocy as combustible and explosive materials stowed adjacent to the heat of boilers.

In the passage of time, talk of the *Erie* and her hopeful immigrants waned . . . all but the saga of Augustus Fuller, her brave wheelsman. Almost immediately he became the stuff of which legends and folklore are forged. The story of Augustus Fuller, sometimes embellished to fit the occasion, made the rounds from pilot house to fo'c'sle, from decks to waterfront taverns, and from pulpits to dinner table and living room discussion. Strangely, however, somewhere in the restating of the tale his first name became Luther, though in truth the only crew member with the given name of Luther was Luther Searles, a fireman subsequently rescued by the *Dewitt Clinton.*

Picking up momentum with the frequent telling and retelling, the tale of the valiant wheelsman was soon the talk of the country and the subject of many editorials and sermons, all of them extolling the virtues of this man who placed the lives of his fellow men above his own. But for Augustus Fuller, or Luther Fuller as some still insisted, it mattered little, for what remained of him was still interred in the charred remains of the *Erie,* which finally succumbed and sank off Silver Creek.

Augustus Fuller ceased to become fact and became legend after a succession of poets and writers took outrageous advantage of their privilege of literary license. The first such opportunist was Charles Dickens, the celebrated English novelist and essayist.

Dickens, who toured the United States in 1842, a year after the *Erie* disaster, found much that displeased him, viewing most of what he witnessed and experienced with a supercilious air, as though constantly exposed to sights, sounds, and smells he deemed offensive. He made a trip from Sandusky to Cleveland on the steamer *Constellation* and, while terming her "handsomely fitted out," he complained that her high-pressure steam boilers gave him a feeling such as might be experienced by lodging on the first floor of a powder mill. He was also caustic and abrasive as to his opinion of Lake Erie, which, he discovered, had "deplorably short seas."

But Charles Dickens was also an imaginative writer, and the tale of Augustus Fuller or Luther Fuller, was prime material for his pen. Subsequently his story, entitled "Helmsman of Lake Erie," was widely printed and reprinted both here and abroad.

Dickens, for reasons that escaped many, for the story stood on its own merits, embellished his yarn with preposterous liberties. He apparently found the hero's name unlikly to inspire sustained interest and renamed him John Maynard, a good English name. He also changed the name of the *Erie* to *Jersey*, added a good forty years to the helmsman's age, and endowed him with virtues Fuller, a mortal man, did not possess. Dickens further distorted the truth by inserting imaginary conversations between the captain and assorted crew members. He even ignored the true source of the blaze and intimated that during the early stages of the conflagration the crew and passengers were called together for the purpose of forming a bucket brigade.

The story enjoyed wide circulation, but in the telling Augustus Fuller had ceased to exist, and a character of fantasy, John Maynard, had emerged as the hero of the ages. But Charles Dickens was an author of international stature and his word was not to be questioned. Those who knew the true story didn't really care, for they knew who the real hero was.

Others followed in Dickens' wake, all serving to perpetuate the legend of the indomitable John Maynard. In the rationalization of the propagandist, that the persistent retelling of a fable makes it gospel, they were highly successful.

John Milton Hay, Lincoln's assistant secretary and biographer and also a writer and poet of note, saw the potential of the bare facts and penned a poem that also found wide acceptance. Jim Bludso was the heroic helmsman, the location the Mississippi River, and the burning steamer the *Prairie Belle,* an old stern-wheeler. But there is little doubt that the tragic *Erie* was the inspiration.

Next Horatio Alger, Jr., a man who achieved fame and fortune writing dime novels had a go at the formula in a poem he authored in 1875. He kept John Maynard but changed the name of the vessel to *Ocean Queen* and had Captain Titus standing beside his helmsman to the very end. He never explained the origin of the fire.

In due time the John Maynard saga reached Europe, where noted poet Theodor Fontane composed his own version. He named the ship the *Swallow*, had her running to Buffalo from Detroit, and made her point of demise a beach near Buffalo, with all saved but the heroic John Maynard. The Fontane version ends with Maynard's flower-covered casket being lowered into a grave near a marble shaft, erected by grateful passengers, where gold letters formed his epitaph:

> Here rests John Maynard.
> He held the wheel firm in his hands
> through smoke and fire.
> He saved us all, he wears a crown,
> he died for us, our love his only reward.

Although Fontane successfully refrained from including any of the true facts or circumstances, his poem won instant admiration, especially in Germany and Bavaria, where individual deeds of bravery, particularly the follow-orders-no-matter-what variety, were held to be most noble. In time the poem became required reading in the secondary schools, and generations of children were obliged to memorize the ten stanzas.

When Hildegard Mund was growing up in Etzenrot, a village in the Abtal Valley, she too had to commit the poem to memory. And in Lubeck, Peter Kroeger likewise had to learn by rote the epic tale. To them John Maynard was one of the great heroes of all time.

Understandably, when Peter and Hildegard were married and came to the United States in 1962, they had priorities based on Theodor Fontane's poem. The first thing they wanted to see was Lake Erie, because that was the lake John Maynard had sailed on. Then they wanted to see Buffalo, because it was on the beach there, according to Fontane's story, that John Maynard had beached his burning ship. Lastly, they wanted to see John Maynard's grave and the marble shaft erected by grateful passengers.

"And then we learned that nobody in America had ever heard of poor John Maynard," sighed Hildegard. "No grave, no shaft, no John Maynard. It is strange, very strange."

Indeed, *wer ist* John Maynard?

2

·
·
·
·

⚓

"Gentlemen, Let Us
Not Be Hasty . . ."

The steamer *Margaret Olwill* [1] was not a vessel of unusual grace or beauty. Her very design involved, quite frankly, shunning some of the aesthetics of shipbuilding in favor of modest costs while achieving a maximum of practicality. Thoroughly conventional of bow and stern, she was built to haul rough cargoes as efficiently as possible, nothing more. She was an uncomplicated vessel and those associated with her navigation, management, and other affairs were mostly uncomplicated people with uncomplicated names such as Brown, Smith, and Jones. Built in Cleveland in the fall of 1887, she was 175 feet long, with her width of 34 feet making her slightly beamier than contemporaries of comparable keel length.

[1] Margaret Olwill was the maiden name of the first wife of Pat Smith, pioneer Cleveland marine contractor and founder of the company that owned the *Margaret Olwill* and a variety of lake craft. His sons, L. P. and J. A. Smith, carried on the family business.

In late June of 1899, a few months before her twelfth birthday, the little steamer was doing precisely what she was properly equipped to do, hauling crushed limestone from the quarries of Kelleys Island, in the western basin of Lake Erie, to Cleveland. There, her owners, L. P. and James A. Smith, had a contract to haul untold tons of such material for the extension of the west arm of Cleveland's harbor breakwater. That project was expected to take eight years, obviously at some profit to the Messrs. Smith. All spring she had shuttled back and forth with the regularity of a scheduled passenger boat. The voyage was just under sixty miles so most of her crew were able to make frequent visits to their homes while the boat was being unloaded. It was a boon not often experienced by the crewmen of other Smith-managed vessels—several schooners, steamers, and the big tug *Chauncey Morgan.*

Skipper of the *Margaret Olwill* was forty-four-year-old Captain John Brown, her master for five years. He was one of six brothers, four of them lake captains, hailing from St. Clair, Michigan, a community along the St. Clair River in an area known to sailors as "the flats." Brother Wesley C. Brown was master of the steamer *North Land;* William Brown commanded the steamer *Westward;* and George Brown was skipper of the steamer *Arrow,* a Cleveland-to-Put-in-Bay excursion vessel. Captain John Brown had garnered some early local fame while still a youth, for his swimming prowess, stroking across the swift and wide St. Clair River with some frequency.

There was more than met the eye in Captain John Brown, a slightly built man whose most distinguished physical features seemed to be a generous crop of wavy dark hair and a rather ample mustache. Friends, without diminishing their respect for him, freely admitted that he was known to be "a close man with a dollar," a trait not usually associated with sailors. As a result of careful management of his earnings he had been able to acquire a small interest in several lake vessels, including the steamer *Pennsylvania* and the excursion boat *Arrow*, brother George's command.

For four of his five years of employ with the Smith interests the captain had maintained a home in Huron, Ohio, but early in the spring of 1899 he had moved his wife and son to Cleveland, taking a rather large apartment house which, fully in keeping with his reputation, he proceeded to fill with paying guests. Nor did the good captain frown on practicing his very useful philosophy of nepotism and cronyism when he was in a position to provide gainful employment. In the crew of eight required to operate the *Margaret Olwill*, wheelsman George Heffron was a cousin of Mrs. Brown and fireman William Doyle, her brother. Second engineer Luke Cynski was an old friend from St. Clair, the captain's boyhood home, as was the chief engineer, Patrick Murphy. Beyond the friend-and-family pale were watchman Frank Hipp, from Kelleys Island, mate John Smith, deckhand Duncan Coyle, and another deckhand whose name, probably because he was not part of the "family," was not even officially recorded in the owner's offices. They remembered that part of it was James but did not know if it was his first name or last.

Captain Brown's day-to-day operating philosophy epitomized a rather unfortunate era on the lakes. It was a period when it was not only unfashionable but also unwise to question the judgment or decisions of owners, no matter how unreasonable or unrealistic they might be. Overloading, safety procedures, and dangerous weather considerations were quite properly the province of captains, but often these decisions were made by men ashore, many of whom had little or no sailing experience themselves. Captain Brown had a reputation for following orders, no matter what, and for that reason he was the kind of man owners preferred. As his friend Captain Russel Jones, a former skipper turned mining expert, observed, "He has been known to overload vessels, sailing when he knew they were overloaded, but the owner had said to do it and Johnny followed instructions."

The only fly in Captain Brown's ointment that late June day when the *Margaret Olwill* departed Cleveland was that chief engineer Patrick Murphy, his old and trusted friend, was not at his accustomed post. The brothers Smith had unceremoniously transferred him to one of the small excursion vessels they operated, steaming to and from downtown Cleveland to Euclid Beach Park, an amusement and resort center on the far east side of the city. Both Captain Brown and engineer Murphy had protested, but to no avail. James A. Smith, the man who made the decision, was adamant and refused to countermand his order. Murphy's place on the *Margaret Olwill* was taken by Alexander McLea, a thoroughly qualified man, but the captain missed the camaradarie that had developed through years of sailing together. He was determined to get Murphy reassigned to his vessel, although he got along well with Mr. McLea.

On this particular voyage, the *Margaret Olwill* was

blessed with another, out-of-the-ordinary situation. Although the owners had not been consulted, the captain had brought along Mrs. Brown, their eleven-year-old son, Blanchard, and a close friend of Mrs. Brown, Mrs. Cora Hitchcock Hunt. Mrs. Hunt had taken the day off from her position at the Hower & Higbee Company, the prominent dry-goods merchants. Mrs. Brown's parents, Mr. and Mrs. James Doyle, had also been invited to make the trip but Mr. Doyle, after visiting the vessel at the dock, declined for both of them.[2]

The Browns were particularly proud of young Blanchard and gave him a full measure of love and devotion. A rather large gilt-framed photograph of him, revealing a shock of dark hair and a shy, wistful smile, occupied a prominent place in the main cabin. Captain Brown frequently pointed out the likeness and commented on his hopes and ambitions for the lad.

The shuttle from Cleveland to Kelleys Island was a series of routine, uncomplicated voyages. On this particular morning the weather was fine, with the vessel rolling gently in a very modest following sea. She kept a respectable distance off the projecting finger off the northeast corner of the island, steering midway between its offshore rocks and Kelleys Island Shoal. A slight deviation of course to port then brought her in, still in deep water, to the north dock of the Kelley Island Lime and Transport Company. The raised dock projected into the lake a respectable distance. It towered above the vessels it served, the crushed lime-

---

2 Mr. Doyle could not exactly define why he declined the invitation for a trip on the *Margaret Olwill*. "It was not quite a premonition," he explained. "It was just that I was not impressed by her."

stone loaded by gravity down chutes from storage "pockets" filled by railroad cars directly from the quarry's crushing facilities.

After his vessel had been positioned at the dock, Captain Brown arranged for a horse and buggy to take the ladies and young Blanchard on a tour of the island. They were shown the village, the ferry dock on the south side, the endless vineyards and, best of all, the famous glacial grooves and Inscription Rocks, where some long-since-vanished race had left intriguing clues of its life and times in pictographs.

The excursion provided pleasant diversion and spared the little group the noise, confusion, and clouds of limestone dust that a fitful northeast wind swirled around the dock and steamer. Meanwhile, Captain Brown took an active interest in the 300 tons of limestone that came rumbling down into his vessel, making sure the tonnage was evenly distributed throughout the hold. In due time the stone was even with the hatch coamings. He then directed the loading of another 600 tons as deck cargo. This was common practice for the stone carriers, and he was merely doing what he and every other master in the trade had been doing for years, although most of them were content with a more modest deckload. But 600 tons, twice that of her hold capacity?

The wind was blowing fresh, still from the northeast, when the *Margaret Olwill* departed her dock at 6:10 P.M. on an otherwise pleasant evening. Two hours later the wind, still from the same quadrant, suddenly grew violent, blowing steadily at what chief engineer McLea estimated to be fifty miles per hour, a fair-to-middlin' gale in any sailor's book. The steamer was making very little headway and rolling considerably. Captain Brown, probably with thoughts of the heavy deck load uppermost in his mind, turned his vessel a point or two directly into the wind and seas. The rolling was somewhat modified but now, with the seas lengthened out after protracted hours of wind from the same direction, the ship began to pitch and pound heavily, taking green water over her bow. Heavily laden and responding slowly to the lift of the seas, the wooden hull worked actively amid a strident chorus of groaning complaints.

At about ten o'clock, engineer McLea ventured into the hold and, finding a few inches of water sloshing about, started up the steam siphons. Returning later to clear them of particles of limestone, he was appalled to find the water almost up to his waist. Investigating quickly, he found two large areas on the starboard side where seams had opened up. And another dangerous leak had developed on the port side. The weight of the deck load, he concluded, after the accumulated punishment of many such loads, had simply been too much for the hull structure. In the parlance of wooden-ship seamen, the *Margaret Olwill* had "sprung her butts."

The little steamer was already showing the effects of the flooding, responding even more sluggishly to the lift of the seas, now rolling again and with agonizingly slow recoveries. The 600-ton deck load of limestone had apparently remained fairly stable at first, but some of it must have shifted, for when engineer McLea went forward to report the massive leaks, the list to port was so severe that he had to crawl on his hands and knees.

In the cabin just below the pilot house he glimpsed the two ladies and little Blanchard, huddled together and obviously very frightened and sick.

News of the ominous state of affairs below caused Captain Brown to clasp his hands to his head and cry, "My God, whatever possessed me to bring my wife and boy with me?"

The captain at first contemplated making a run for shelter at Lorain, but he feared the vessel would not stay afloat that long. McLea flatly predicted that they had a half hour, perhaps not that much time. "Maybe we could beach her," he suggested.

There was really no choice, although the chances of the steamer reaching shore, eight miles to starboard, were next to nothing. But it was, as it has always been, the master's decision. "Hard astarboard," he ordered wheelsman Heffron.

But turning the vessel toward shore necessarily involved exposing her to the merciless troughs of the seas. In a normally laden steamer it would have been foolhardy at best. But with the vessel already "tender" because of the big deck load, it was madness. But again, what was the alternative?

Rolling drunkenly, she tried to respond to her rudder and thrashing propeller, coming about ever so painfully to lie there between the rising mountains of water, wallowing, creaking, and groaning as the thundering seas assaulted her broadside. The strain upon her steering chains proved too much. Suddenly the wheel in Heffron's hand spun uselessly. The chains had parted. The wheelsman, sensing that the break was near the fantail, fought his way to the stern to see if repairs could be effected. He encountered the aft crew preparing to abandon ship in the lifeboat, for it was apparent without the captain pointing out the fact that the *Margaret Olwill* was doomed.

Deckhand Duncan Coyle, convinced that he was in for a bit of swimming, was trying to get his shoes off. He had cast one aside but was having difficulty with the laces of the other. "Cut it off," someone shouted. He whipped out his knife and had just slashed the laces when he was struck by a loose cask catapulted from its cradle by the violent rolling of the steamer. The cask and Coyle went over the side together.

The *Margaret Olwill* was designed to carry a heavy, dense cargo, but deep down in her hold, not pyramided on deck over the burden that already filled her to her hatch coamings. It was the shifting mountain of crushed limestone that finished her, the tremendous weight heeling her over, first to port and then to starboard, rails under with every roll and the recoveries painfully slow and harrowing.

First mate John Smith was in the pilot house when, at 11:15 P.M., the end came. He saw a great sea rise on the starboard side, rolling the *Margaret Olwill* heavily to port. During the brief second the vessel lay in the trough he heard Captain Brown belatedly shout "Man the boats" and saw him dash into the cabin to get the ladies and young Blanchard. It was an order that should have been given sooner, much sooner, assuming that a boat could have been launched under the prevailing circumstances. Even so the mate heard a chorus of screams as the ladies were told the news. Mate Smith then saw another huge sea mounting from the port side. This time the deckload

slid to the starboard in an awful, relentless rush, and the
Margaret Olwill flipped over like a pancake.

Mate Smith, who had been unsuccessfully trying to find
a life preserver, went over with her, never expecting to
come up. But he did, fortunately popping up through a
window that had once been part of a cedar partition between the captain's cabin and an adjoining one. As she
went over, the seas had wiped off the vessel's superstructure
as effectively as a charge of dynamite. Smith saw Mrs.
Hunt thrashing about, but only briefly. Soon she was gone.
He spotted watchman Frank Hipp and shouted for the
fireman to join him on the wreckage. Hipp answered in
some unintelligible words but went under before he could
swim the short distance.

At first there had been other shouts, cries, and pleadings
but they were quickly muted and overpowered by the clamorous breaking seas and the howl of the gale. Some apparently perished in seconds or moments . . . little Blanchard, Captain and Mrs. Brown, Cora Hitchcock Hunt,
fireman William Doyle, and the deckhand James, whose
full name was neither recorded on the records ashore nor
remembered by his shipmates.

Dawn, breaking reluctantly it seemed to those who still
lived, revealed a still tumultuous sea, a massive, scattered
field of tossing wreckage, and two small groups of survivors,
separated by nearly a mile, each unaware of the other.

Duncan Coyle and wheelsman George Heffron were
clinging to a section of the deckhouse. It was small, scarcely
bore their weight, and was swept over by every sea. A mile
to the east, the other group, clutching the cabin partition
Smith had found so handily, was comprised of Smith, en-

gineer McLea, and second engineer Luke Cynski. They, too, were temporarily submerged by each sea, suffering from the cold, and growing weaker as the long night hours passed. Mate Smith had already resigned himself to the fact that, even if they survived, they would not be rescued in time for him to attend the regular Thursday meeting of his fraternal order, Hesperian Lodge, Knights of Pythias. He had previously planned to join his lodge brothers while the *Margaret Olwill*, had she kept to schedule, would have been unloading.

The spirits of the three suddenly came alive when, shortly after dawn, they saw a big, broad-beamed steamboat bearing down almost upon them. The very practical Luke Cynski had snatched up a piece of canvas for just such an occasion. He somehow wrapped it around a stick from the wreckage and waved frantically. All three, although they were weak from exposure, shouted until they were hoarse. But the light was still dim, the seas confusing. Aboard the *State of Ohio*, Captain Willoughby, master, their plight went unnoticed, although several people were visible on the steamer's deck and the normal complement of officers was on watch. Maddened with frustration and thoroughly disheartened, the trio cursed and pounded on their makeshift raft in utter despair.

Ten minutes later the *State of Ohio* came upon a considerably larger field of wreckage. Captain Willoughby checked his steamer, and all hands and passengers crowded the rails, looking for survivors. Someone spotted Coyle and Heffron clinging to their bit of wreckage, a piece so insubstantial that it barely kept their heads above water.

Indeed, as the seas swept over them they temporarily disappeared.

Captain Willoughby was forced to turn his vessel and work his way into the heaving wreckage with great care, fearful of damaging the buckets on the big sidewheels. Slowly he eased the big steamer close to where the two men were clinging desperately to their makeshift life preserver, too numb with cold and exhaustion to call out. High seas and the tumbling flotsam ruled out any attempt to launch a lifeboat. From the apparent condition of the pair, time would not have permitted such a maneuver. Lines were thrown to them accurately. But it was too late for George Heffron. He slipped out of sight as a rope splashed down within easy reach. Duncan Coyle, however, revived enough to wrap a line about his waist and was hauled aboard the passenger steamer.

Ironically, the three sailors the *State of Ohio* had unwittingly bypassed witnessed the rescue operation. Frantically they again shouted at the top of their voices, but to no avail.

Coyle, in a bizarre twist of circumstances, really owed his life to the severity of the storm. The *State of Ohio* had been scheduled to leave her Cleveland dock at nine o'clock the previous evening, and had she done so would have passed the wreckage in total darkness with scarcely a chance of seeing the two sailors or even becoming aware that there had been a shipwreck. The very intensity of the weather that Wednesday night had impelled her owners, the Cleveland & Buffalo Navigation Company, to hold her in port until three o'clock Thursday morning. Altogether, counting the hour spent coming about to rescue Coyle, the *State of Ohio* was over six hours late making her Toledo dock.[3]

Seemingly abandoned to their fate, albeit unknowingly, by the good Captain Willoughby, mate Smith and engineers McLea and Cynski were about done in, mentally and physically. Bitter, their hopes dashed, and almost drained of strength, they still clung tenaciously to their little island of wreckage. Around them the flotsam that had once been part of their steamer rose and fell with the same seas that still washed over them.

Cynski was the first to spot it . . . another vessel bearing down and on a course that would obviously take her near them. Engineer McLea suggested that they not waste strength and voice. "We'll all yell at the same time, and that way they'll have a better chance of hearing us," he counseled.

When the steamer came abreast they did just as he had asked. For a few heart-rending moments it seemed that their hoarse shouts, raised in unison, had again been in vain. But then, wonderfully, the vessel's whistle gave out a series of throaty roars, her propeller began to thrash astern and the sore beset sailors knew that they had been sighted. This time they again pounded their makeshift raft, but in sheer joy.

The large steamer turned out to be the *Sacramento*, out of Bay City, Michigan, Captain James F. Bowen, in com-

[3] Several days after the *Margaret Olwill* foundered the late Captain Frank E. Hamilton was in the pilot house of the steamer *Arrow*, commanded by Captain George Brown. As the vessel steamed northward from the Cedar Point piers, it passed through a considerable quantity of wreckage. Included in the flotsam, clearly visible, was the nameboard from the *Margaret Olwill*'s pilot house. Neither man spoke, but Captain Hamilton later recalled that tears coursed down the cheeks of Captain Brown.

mand. Captain Bowen had sighted the wreckage, but visibility was so poor he would have passed the trio of survivors but for their hallooing. But the *Sacramento*, of the Davidson fleet, was a large vessel and did not handle smartly in the high seas and wind. Captain Bowen did considerable backing and filling as he tried to work his steamer around to keep the victims in his lee. He ordered a boat lowered and put it in charge of his chief engineer, this in itself highly unusual.

At nearby Lorain, the *Sacramento*'s curious maneuverings attracted the attention of the crew aboard the harbor tug *Cascade*. Fearing that the vessel was encountering trouble and possibly in distress, Captain Mansfield, the tug's skipper, put out to render whatever help his tug could provide. Literally corkscrewing through quartering seas, the tug made rather slow progress, but as she neared the scene the reason for the *Sacramento*'s strange behavior became obvious. The lifeboat had already picked up one man but was having difficulty reaching the other two. The *Cascade*, more agile in the nasty seas, steamed into the wreckage to take off the other two. Then, after relieving the lifeboat of its shivering passenger, Captain Mansfield directed a brief search with all hands looking sharply for more victims. Meanwhile, in the warmth of the tug's boiler room, mate Smith and engineers McLea and Cynski made a rapid recovery.

The *State of Ohio*, immediately upon docking at Toledo, wired to Cleveland the news of the wreck and the apparent loss of all hands except Duncan Coyle. This news quickly hit the streets with the very next edition of the Cleveland newspapers. Dispatches from Lorain, listing the other three survivors, did not get to Cleveland in time to make the same afternoon editions. But when it was later learned that others had been picked up, Mrs. McLea departed at once for Lorain, just about the time her husband boarded another train for Cleveland. Somewhere in the twenty-five miles between the cities they passed.

Among those most profoundly affected by the news of the *Margaret Olwill*'s foundering was Patrick Murphy, Captain Brown's favorite engineer, who was moved to fall upon his knees and give thanks to his Creator and J. A. Smith, not necessarily in that order, for his transfer from the ill-fated steamer and his subsequent deliverance from the Grim Reaper.

The marine fraternity, shocked by the loss of a staunch and relatively new vessel, recalled many tales of the frugal captain and his philosophy of always following orders, no matter what.

"He knew only one thing, and that was to follow orders," commented his old friend, Captain Jones. "He was a fearless fellow, often the first one out in the spring and the last one to turn in at winter. If the owners had told him to put the boat on the beach, he would have done it."

When a shift of the wind and a warm sun had quieted the seas, Harvey Hill, from a modest bluff along Lorain's east side, spotted a field of wreckage working in toward the shore. Pulling for it in his boat he found part of the pilot house, the bridge, and a water tank. He was about to start for shore with the tank when he discovered the body of a woman entangled in a cluster of wood and cordage. It proved to be Cora Hitchcock, Mrs. Brown's friend.

Later in the day Frank Kelley, another salvager, probed

the flotsam wandering in to the beach. Among the items he picked up were a trunk, bureau, odds and ends of personal belongings, and a gilt picture frame containing a portrait of a young boy with a shock of dark hair and a shy, wistful smile.

Mate John Smith, definitely a creature of habit, was not deterred from doing what he had planned to do when the *Margaret Olwill* made port—attend the weekly meeting of Hesperian Lodge, Knights of Pythias. His concerned lodge brothers, however, had not been apprised of late dispatches and, under the assumption that he had indeed perished, were soberly discussing plans for his funeral and preparing a resolution of condolence for his next of kin. Although it was not characteristic of him, being somewhat of an introvert, Smith could not resist the dramatic opportunity so unexpectedly thrust upon him. He strode past the speechless outer guard in the anteroom, grinned at his lodge brothers and said, "Gentlemen, let us not be hasty about sending me on my way. At this time I must decline your well-meant proposal!"

3

⚓

"From Labor Below
to Refreshment Above"

A good shipmaster, whatever his reputation as a seaman, best represents his owners and his own good character by the friends he makes ashore. And Captain Homer Beardsley of the schooner *W. W. Arnold* was a gentleman held in high esteem not only by the sailors who worked under him, but by the shoreside men with whom he conducted the ship's business. He was a man who almost immediately inspired confidence and a desire to know him better.

During the season of 1868, when master of the bark *Fontanelle*, he developed warm friendships with businessmen in Munising, Michigan, in the state's Upper Peninsula, on the still primitive south shore of Lake Superior. It was an era of booming iron and copper exploration and development. After hauling ore to lower lakes ports, principally Cleveland, the *Fontanelle* and other craft often returned with mining machinery, industrial equipment, coal, or the myriad supplies needed by the businesses and citizens of communities literally isolated from civilization during the long winter months. Always there was that cargo of iron ore for the return voyage, loaded at nearby Marquette, already looked upon as the capital of the new and mushrooming industry.

On the occasion of several voyages to Munising, Captain Beardsley had become fast friends with David Sang, superintendent of Munising Township; J. S. Wood; A. S. Perinier; and J. T. McCullam, the township clerk. Beyond their business and social meetings, the five were bound together by the mystic ties of membership in the Masonic Order. The local men were delighted to discover that Captain Beardsley was a member of Bigelow Lodge in Cleveland. And they were happy for him when, early in 1869, he was given command of a newer and larger vessel, the schooner *W. W. Arnold*.

The *W. W. Arnold*, only six years old and said to be an exceptionally staunch vessel, was built in Buffalo and was recorded as a 426-ton craft. She was owned and managed by John D. Bothwell of the Cleveland firm of Bothwell & Ferris, dock owners and iron ore merchants. Mr. Bothwell had achieved some fame as the inventor of a steam-driven device to replace horses and mules in lifting large, hand-loaded buckets of ore from vessel cargo holds. His invention created favorable comment in the industry, and he promptly had several more built. However, he must have been a cold, heartless man, as we will learn, despite his business acumen and inventive bent.

At four o'clock on the afternoon of November 4, 1869, the *Arnold* departed Marquette burdened with 550 tons of iron ore. She had carried as much as 650 tons, but it was late in the season and Captain Beardsley, a prudent mariner, decided that the additional freeboard of the lighter load might stand him in good stead. In addition to her master and a crew of eight, the *Arnold* had two passengers, one a gentleman whose name the dock men did not ascertain, the other Willie Boyes, a part-time Marquette post office worker returning for the winter to the home of his parents in St. Clair, Michigan. The departure was routine and orderly, and soon observers ashore could see all the schooner's canvas going up.

Four hours after the *Arnold* cast off her lines, Lake Superior fell under the malignant influence of a powerful northwest storm spawned in the prairie provinces of Canada. It boomed down over Thunder Bay, raked the flanks of the Sleeping Giant, and whistled onward over Isle Royale, building up in intensity over the broadening lake. It was, as sailors are wont to say, "a fierce gale of wind," this one accompanied by plummeting temperatures and blinding snow. As the awesome combination of wind, towering seas, and blizzard ravished Lake Superior, keeper Ashman of the Whitefish Point Light remarked to his assistant that it was the worst storm he had witnessed in all his years of duty. North of Marquette, on Granite Island, a stunned and frightened keeper sought shelter and watched unbelievingly as the raging wind stripped the metal sheathing from the lighthouse tower there. Matchi Manito, the evil spirit of the Chippewas, was afoot on Lake Superior that night, and in Marquette many prayers were said for the ships and sailors exposed to his wrath out on the open lake.

But the *Arnold* never arrived at Sault Ste. Marie (the

Soo), where she would have had to transit the ship canal en route to her lower lakes destination of Cleveland. Lock workers reported no sighting of her nor did the many up-bound vessels arriving at Marquette. Some sailing craft, being apprised of the schooner's overdue status, deliberately coasted along, nearer than usual to the rugged shoreline, hoping to sight her stranded hull. True, the topmasts of a vessel were found on a beach near Whitefish Point, but they were believed to be from the schooner *Milan*, lost some weeks earlier near that location.

The Marquette *Mining Journal*, then a weekly and ever conscious of the rapport the community had with the ships that called at its doorstep and the men who sailed them, duly reported the glum prognosis of those who searched, at the same time holding out a vain hope that the *Arnold* had merely been damaged and was anchored or ashore in some remote area. The paper suggested that perhaps, being unable to make Whitefish Point and gain its shelter, the *Arnold* had been driven over to the Canadian side of the lake and had possibly rounded Corbeil Point to anchor in lonely Batchawana Bay. There, assuming that all her canvas had been lost in the storm, she might be helpless. But when twelve days had passed with no heartening word of the missing schooner, even the *Mining Journal* concluded that this fact "causes the most fearful apprehensions to be entertained."

In Cleveland, the *Mining Journal* reported, the loss of the *Arnold* was quickly discredited because of the ability and experience of Captain Beardsley, the staunchness of the vessel, and her superior sea-going characteristics. Some of this optimism might have been inspired as a result of an erroneous dispatch from Detroit which had officers of the *Adriatic* reporting the *Arnold* ashore and a total loss at Vermilion Point, ten miles west of Whitefish Point, the crew safe. This was at once repudiated by the captain and mates of the steamer *Northern Light,* also moored at Detroit. What or who originated the cruel and completely inaccurate report was never revealed.

Ship owners of the day, beyond determining that their vessel's insurance papers were in order, rarely evinced emotion or concern over the fate of crews. Nor did the disappearance of the *Arnold* inspire any pity or compassion in the heart of her owner, John D. Bothwell. Never, during the days when anxious seamen and shipmasters were looking for her, did he or any emissary acting for him take part in the search or offer any encouragement, financial or otherwise. Less than a month after the *Arnold* departed her Marquette dock, he abandoned his interest in the vessel to the underwriters, collected his insurance, and surrendered her title to them. They, presuming any wreckage was ever found, could then dispose of the fittings and salvageable material for whatever the market would bring.

Ironically, on the same day her owners were reported abandoning the vessel to the underwriters, came the first positive word as to the fate of the *Arnold*. With primitive roads in the Upper Peninsula becoming impassable in bad weather, residents of Munising, Marquette, and other communities relied upon overland mail carriers from Sault Ste. Marie who, when the snow lay deep, made the trip with dog sled or snowshoes, generally following the lake shore. It was a circuitous route, but it was also infinitely better than braving the wolf packs of the forests. One of the mail

carriers arrived at Munising with the report that he had
sighted the hull of a large, dark-colored vessel lying broadside on the beach just where the Big Two Hearted River
made its junction with Lake Superior. It was, he stated,
badly broken up, dismasted, and with her yawl boat shattered and cast up on the beach. The site was twenty-five
miles west of Whitefish Point and about fifty-five miles
east of Munising. "There can be no doubt that this is the
Arnold," reported the *Mining Journal*, "as it answers her
description and she is the only missing vessel on the lake."

A second mail carrier arrived days later at Marquette,
verifying the wreck and giving a few additional details.
The wrecked hull, he stated, had been wiped clean of
everything on deck except the windlass and stem. The terrible fury of the storm that claimed the schooner was dram-
atized by the fact that most of the wreckage beyond the
hull itself was on top of a bluff, thirty or forty feet above
the lake and several rods beyond the sand beach. He spotted
the roof of a cabin, rope lines, provision boxes, furniture,
bedding, and the demolished yawl. Neither mail carrier
came closer to the wreck than the bluff, nor did they look
for bodies, a situation the *Mining Journal* attributed to
the fact that both men were Indians and deemed contact
with dead persons as an omen of evil. The mail carrier did
report, however, that he had encountered a trapper who
told him that he had passed along the beach three days
after the storm and saw ten bodies lying at the edge of the
water.

But the rituals of the Masonic order were not taken
lightly by the good friends Captain Beardsley left behind
in Munising. One of the obligations of the order is one

that commands personal sacrifice to relieve a brother in distress. Accordingly, Messrs. Sang, Wood, McCullam, and Perinier departed Munising, determined to at least provide a Christian burial for their lost lodge brother, if they could find him, and also for any other members of the crew.

Accompanied by a trusty Indian voyageur as a guide they attempted to make the trip by small boat, but shortly after leaving the harbor they found Lake Superior to be in an inhospitable mood. They abandoned the boat and donned snowshoes, camping out two nights before reaching the cabin of Michael Blucher at Grand Marais. During the course of a welcome meal Mr. Blucher stated that the storm that claimed the *Arnold* was the worst within his memory. At one time, he reported, the fierce wind raised the water in the harbor four feet, floating the barrels of salt in his fish house and damaging his property in general.

Commandeering an abandoned skiff, the lodge brothers attempted to row the rest of the way, but, with night coming on, they selected a landing place between the shorefast icebergs and camped out yet another night. Early the next morning they proceeded by foot, arriving at the wreck scene before noon. They had heard so much about the *Arnold*'s staunch construction that they were unprepared for what they found.

Mr. Sang, in his report to the *Mining Journal,* recounted the scene.

We began to look for evidences of the wreck, and we found them to be quite numerous, in the shape of small bits of canvas, shirts, coats, socks, and similar items which we cut out of the ice and saved, but on none of them could we find any mark or name by which they might be identified. Here we would say that the scene that presented itself was so entirely different from what we expected that we almost doubted the possibility of its being the wreck of the *Arnold*. She was literally torn to atoms and cast high and dry upon the beach.[1] We immediately began searching in the heap of ruins for her name. Mr. Mc-Cullam was the first to discover the name when he found a piece of her bulwarks with the inscription thereon. We all crowded around there to read for ourselves, *W. W. Arnold*. We felt that it would have been impossible for any person to have reached the shore alive, and that our brother Beardsley, has been called from "labor below to refreshment above." And although a thorough search was made for bodies, nothing was found but pillows, mattresses, the wreckage of the ship's furniture, and the back of the captain's armchair. It was agreed that the recovery of any of the victims must wait until spring for the entire beach area was a mass of ice and a substantial snow cover which prevented an efficient search.

Mr. McCullam did pick up a glove that he was certain was one of a pair Captain Beardsley was wearing the night before the *Arnold* departed Marquette.

The gallant searchers returned without accomplishing their mission of giving Captain Beardsley and his men a Christian burial, but vowed that they would return to faithfully discharge their sacred fraternal duty.

Upon their arrival back in Munising, they received another bit of intelligence. Another mail carrier had found

[1] The terribly splintered wreckage of the *Arnold* may not have been entirely the result of the storm that finished her. Although a major blow in any seaman's experience, it did not cover a large geographic area of the lakes. After the *Arnold* had gone missing, but before her wreck was discovered and reported, the entire Great Lakes chain was swept by a monstrous three-day gale during which ninety-seven vessels foundered or stranded. Helpless there on the beach, the *Arnold*'s hull would have been torn asunder.

the ship's compass, cast up on the beach, and had taken it back to Sault Ste. Marie with him.

The following April the *Mining Journal* received a dispatch from Messrs. Trempe and Taylor of Sault Ste. Marie to the effect that they had visited the wreck site and had found a body they believed to be that of Captain Beardsley, identified as such by the fact that the clothing contained a bill from a Chicago firm for ship's stores and rope. They buried the remains on high land and marked the grave so it could be located later. Like the previous visitors, the Trempe party found part of the *Arnold* on one side of the river, a section of the forward bulwarks on the opposite side with a large hawser attached. They also found the bottom of the vessel, with the ore still in it, lying in about ten feet of water, with the anchors, windlass, chains, and head rigging all in a heap. An incidental and somewhat pathetic recovery was that of a handkerchief marked "W. H. Boyes." Poor Willie Boyes had shared the fate of the *Arnold*'s captain and crew. And still another body was discovered and buried.

The Trempe party had been authorized by the underwriters to recover and transport to Munising any fixtures, gear, or fittings of value. Accordingly they brought back a boatload of hawsers, blocks, bolts, and chain and arranged to salvage the anchors.

In a business sense the affairs of the *Arnold* were expeditiously and neatly wrapped up. The grieving families of her master, crew, and passengers were another matter. Owners, once the underwriters had paid off the loss, were not disposed to lavish money or sympathy upon those the sailors left behind, and Mr. Bothwell was no exception. The dead and missing were victims of the times and circumstances that made ships and sailors expendable. Lost men and vessels were more often remembered by others, usually landsmen who dreamed of tall ships, deep water, and filling sails. One of them, a Mr. Mead of Marquette, penned an eighteen stanza poem in memory of the *Arnold* and her crew. It was duly published, with gratitude, by the *Mining Journal*. It ended thus:

> A requiem now we'll sing to the dead,
> Drowned in the fresh water sea,
> Praying that each one's soul hath fled
> To rest, in eternity.

4

⚓

"Let The Lower Lights
Be Burning!"

The name of Philip P. Bliss will never rank among those of great navigators, skippers, Lloyd's Medal winners, or shipping magnates. Yet it is doubtful if any man ever did more to awaken public interest and sympathy to the plight of storm-driven mariners and to the scarcity and fragility of navigational aids at their disposal in times of stress.

During an era when parlor organs provided an outlet for musical self-expression and the social, recreational, and religious activities of neighborhood churches figured prominently in family plans, Bliss enjoyed an enviable household reputation as one of America's great singing evangelists, his name respected by all.

He was best known for his golden-voiced renditions of hymns he himself had composed. So beautiful and emotional was his delivery that tears would often stream from his eyes, and his audiences frequently reacted likewise.

Many of the prolific composer's works soon became standard offerings in most hymnals, as they still are today. So in demand were his services that Bliss spent much of his time making guest appearances at revival meetings sponsored by other famed evangelists such as Dwight L. Moody, D. W. Whittle, and Ira D. Sankey. His name on the advance program almost always guaranteed a full house.

It was at these meetings, listening to the sermons of others, that Bliss often received his inspiration for hymns that soon became favorites of congregations all over the country. A sermon by a Reverend Brundage induced him to write "Almost Persuaded." A message in a service by D. W. Whittle in Chicago, and the evangelist's story of a Civil War battle, inspired his theme for "Hold the Fort." It is believed that other sermons provided the motivation for the writing of "What Shall the Harvest Be?" and "Whosoever Will."

But it was the renowned evangelist Dwight L. Moody, a close personal friend, who gave Bliss the idea for the hymn that made him the favorite of sailors and all the near and dear who waited patiently for ships and men to come home. The scene was again Chicago, in Moody's famed Tabernacle.

The sermon dwelt on the message the evangelist had received by listening to the experiences of a friend, a passenger on a storm-wracked steamer desperately trying to make the shelter of Cleveland harbor on a dark, tempestuous night.[1]

---

[1] Moody's impression, possibly in error, was that the shipwreck occurred at the entrance to Cleveland's harbor, although records of that era make no mention of such a dread event.

Moody related to his faithful followers how many lives were lost because the lower lights along the shore, marking the harbor entrance, were out and only the large light from the lighthouse was burning. The pilot was certain of his general direction but could not see the rocks along the dangerous approach.[2] Concluded Moody, "Brethren, the Master will take care of the great lighthouse; let us keep the lower lights burning!"

Inspired once more, the gifted Bliss came to the next service and sang a new hymn for Moody's eager congregation, "Let the Lower Lights Be Burning!"

> Brightly beams our Father's mercy
> From his lighthouse evermore;
> But to us He gives the keeping
> Of the lights along the shore.
> Dark the night of sin has settled,
> Loud the angry billows roar;
> Eager eyes are watching, longing,
> For the lights along the shore.
> Trim your feeble lamp, my brother!
> Some poor sailor, tempest-tossed,
> Trying to make the harbor,
> In the darkness may be lost.

[Refrain:]

> Let the lower lights be burning!
> Send a gleam across the wave!
> Some poor fainting, struggling seaman
> You may rescue, you may save.

[2] There were no rocks in the vicinity of the harbor entrance, but Moody's informant could possibly have meant the harbor's east pier, which was constructed in 1869. Oil lights marking such obstructions were frequently early victims of high seas and wind. The lighthouse, on the bluff, had been rebuilt in 1872.

The new hymn, published in 1871, affirmed his position as being among the world's foremost composers of such inspiring material. It was soon included in new hymnals and was translated and printed in many languages, eventually including Chinese. "Let the Lower Lights Be Burning" quickly became an international spiritual tribute to the men of the lakes and sea and their perilous lot in life.

His place in the world of religious music assured, his star still in the ascendant, Philip P. Bliss and his good wife were Chicago-bound on the Lake Shore & Michigan Southern Railway's crack *Pacific Express* on the night of Friday, December 29, 1876. The train, originating in New York City, was laboring westward out of Erie, Pennsylvania, two and one-half hours late.

The gospel singer, his wife, and two young sons had spent the Christmas holidays with his parents in Towanda, New York. Scheduled to appear with Dwight L. Moody at his Chicago Tabernacle on Sunday, Bliss had arranged to leave the couple's two sons, Paul and George, with his parents for a few days. The train, Number 5 in railroad parlance, a combined Chicago-Montreal express, had left New York on time. At Albany the Montreal section was detached. The Chicago cars then continued westward, encountering steadily deteriorating weather conditions.[3]

By the time the train departed Erie—next stop Ashtabula, Ohio—icy tracks and a twenty-inch snowfall piled in drifts by high winds had slowed the pace considerably. But the two locomotives, *Socrates*, Dan McGuire at the throttle,

[3] Strangely, the Montreal-bound section of Number 5, detached at Albany, New York, also came to grief and also at a bridge. Near Rutland, Vermont, it derailed and struck a wooden bridge. Both bridge and train tumbled into an icy stream. Luckily there were no fatalities.

and the *Columbia*, "Pap" Folsom similarly employed, plowed on into the teeth of a raging blizzard. Behind them were eleven cars, four for baggage and express, two coaches, a smoker, a parlor car, and three sleepers. It was deluxe equipment with plush seats and woodwork ornamented with gilt and high polish. Oil lamps cast a mellow glow, and coal stoves kept the passengers, still in a holiday mood, warm and comfortable.

It was an era when most railroad passenger cars carried specific names. In the *Yokohama*, the car behind the smoker, the Blisses sat side by side. Someone recalled that Mr. Bliss was often referred to as "the sweet singer of Israel" and noted that he was reading his Bible. But none of those aboard the *Pacific Express* could be expected to know that the last song he had sung in his most recent Moody Tabernacle appearance would prove to be prophetic:

> I know not the hour when my
> Lord will come.
> To take me away to his own dear
> home;
> But I know that His presence will
> lighten the gloom.
> And that will be glory for me!

Dan McGuire, clutching the throttle of the *Socrates*, could have used a few lower lights himself that terrible night. Ahead was the bridge spanning the Ashtabula River, 150 feet long and towering 70 feet over the stream. It was a Howe truss design bridge, the first ever built of iron, planned by Amasa Stone, a stubborn, hard-headed man who was president of the railroad line when the bridge was built in 1865. It was a two-track structure replacing a single-track span of wood. Stone had designed similar bridges of wood and all had been successful. Other qualified engineers had disagreed with him about an iron bridge of the same type, but Stone would brook no dissent.

Joseph Tomlinson, a civil engineer, was given the assignment of preparing the drawings, but upon protesting the proposed bridge's design weaknesses he was driven from Stone's office. Two subordinates, neither of whom had any experience with iron bridge construction, were placed in charge of raising the bridge. Eventually the responsibility of the bridge became that of Charles Collins, chief engineer and bridge inspector of the line, although he never considered it anything but "Mr. Stone's bridge." [4]

Engineer McGuire missed the "slow" warning indicating the approach to the bridge simply because the blizzard was so intense that trackside signals were obliterated by the swirling snow. It really mattered little, because the speed of the *Pacific Express* had been slowed to between ten to fifteen miles per hour due to the slippery tracks and building drifts.

Just as the *Socrates* reached the far or western end of the bridge, McGuire felt the tracks sinking beneath him. Instinctively, he slammed the throttle forward and the locomotive surged ahead to safe ground. However, looking behind him, he saw the *Columbia* strike the stone abutment and fall, and before the coupling broke, the first express car dropped forward under the *Columbia*'s tender. The

---

[4] Although Amasa Stone accepted full responsibility for the bridge design and its subsequent collapse, Charles Collins, chief engineer and bridge inspector, apparently suffered great remorse and took his own life less than a month after the disaster.

Columbia rolled and crashed down upon the express car. On they came, the express cars, the coaches, the smoker, the *Yokohama, Palatine, Osceola,* and the *City of Buffalo,* all piling up in the gorge. Almost immediately fires, started by the overhead oil lights and glowing-hot coal stoves in the train cars, broke out in the jumbled wreckage and spread with frightening rapidity.

Engineer McGuire blew his whistle frantically to summon help, but the efforts of local citizens who struggled down the embankment in heavy snow and the exertions of an inadequate and inefficient volunteer fire department were but token gestures. Trapped in the wreckage and doomed were ninety-two passengers. Another sixty-four were injured, some grievously.[5]

They never knew for sure which of the incinerated bodies were those of Philip P. Bliss and his wife. Short days after the disaster a mile-long public funeral procession trudged through heavy snow and under a leaden sky to inter the coffins of nineteen unidentified victims in a mass grave at Ashtabula's Chestnut Grove Cemetery.[6]

Who knows what hymns were sung at the services, but it would have been entirely fitting had the mourners rendered the hymn that became the favorite of sailors, in honor of the man who himself had just embarked on the great and final voyage.

[5] Two investigations were ordered immediately, one by a local coroner's jury, the other by an Ohio State Legislature special committee. Both ruled the cause to be defective construction, the blame entirely that of the Lake Shore & Michigan Southern Railway. Some bridge experts wondered that the bridge lasted as long as it did.

[6] Some time after the disaster, an obelisk was erected at the site of the mass burial in Chestnut Grove Cemetery. Curious visitors in this age of nostalgia frequently point out the name Philip P. Bliss, chiseled in the marble.

Let the lower lights be burning!
Send a gleam across the wave!
Some poor fainting, struggling seaman
You may rescue, you may save.

The Sad Saga of the *Soo City*—

In the summer of 1908, when Felix Jackson of Velasco, Texas, sought out a vessel for a passenger and freight service he proposed to operate between New Orleans and various Texas ports, he steered a steady course for the Great Lakes. His logic was unassailable. Any saltwater ship of the size he required and at a price he could afford was bound to be aged and undoubtedly afflicted with the scourge of most such craft—a bad bottom due to the insidious workings of the dread teredo or shipworms. New bottoms, copper-sheathed to inhibit the worms, were ruinously expensive. Better, he figured, to buy an old, but sound freshwater vessel, sheathe her worm-free bottom with copper, and count on many more years of service.

Mr. Jackson browsed the waterfronts of several lake ports, particularly those of Lake Michigan, where, through the years, a score or more steamboat companies vied for the passenger, freight, and excursion trade. Boats changed owners, operators, and routes with some frequency as those charged with their management sought out new business, conceived customer-pleasing schedules, and advertised their vessels as the ultimate in comfort, appointments, and speed.

After much looking, inspecting, and the usual haggling, Felix Jackson settled on the twenty-year-old wooden passenger, freight, and excursion steamer *Soo City*, property of the Indiana Transportation Company and operating between Chicago and her home port of Michigan City, Indiana. Still sound, she was available as the season of 1908 was drawing to a close only because her owners were expecting spring delivery of a new vessel, the *United States*.

Built by the F. W. Wheeler Company in West Bay City, Michigan, in 1888, the *Soo City* was slightly over 171 feet long, driven by a 600-horsepower fore-and-aft compound engine, and grossed 670 tons.

When the newly christened steamer arrived at Sault Ste. Marie, Michigan, her namesake city, on her maiden voyage, officials and newspaper people, noting her twenty-one carpeted staterooms, upholstered chairs, stained glass, and mahogany furnishings, immediately pronounced her the "most elegant" of lake vessels. It was a phrase somewhat loosely applied to each new steamer that came out.

Despite the high hopes of her owners, the *Soo City* soon fell into the more or less vagabond status of her many competitors because of fluctuating economic conditions. Built originally for the Delta Transportation Company for the St. Ignace, Mackinac, Cheboygan, and the Soo route, she later, under various owners or charter operators, in several colors or combinations of colors, served on established routes and schedules from Chicago to St. Joseph, Milwaukee, Michigan City, Holland, South Haven, and Muskegon. In 1906 she ventured into Lake Superior, carrying passengers and freight between Duluth and Port Arthur, Ontario. Over the years she received various interior modifications, and was extensively rebuilt in 1900.

In early February of 1907, her owners of record, A. Booth & Company, sold her to the Indiana Transportation Company for service once more between Michigan City and Chicago. So she was back in familiar waters when Mr. Jackson and the Indiana Transportation Company came to an agreement.

Mr. Jackson was not one to let grass grow under his feet. As soon as the deal was concluded, he arranged with the Indiana Transportation Company to sail the vessel to New Orleans, under the charge of some of the men who had comprised her Michigan City–to–Chicago crew. She required only a skeleton crew, really—about fourteen men, as compared to the twenty-eight she normally carried. He also instructed his New York agent, T. H. Franklin, to arrange for drydocking, a general refitting, and the application of copper sheathing on her bottom.

The *Soo City* left Michigan City on November first, under command of her veteran skipper, Captain Frank V. Dority, of South Haven, Michigan.[1] First mate John Casey and second mate Angus McIntyre, both of Chicago, stood their regular pilot house watches. First engineer Charles Warwick was from Michigan City and shared engine-room duties with Chicagoan N. J. Duncan, second engineer.

1 Lake captains in the passenger and excursion trade often became popular figures, ashore or afloat. Captain Frank V. Dority was no exception. During his career he also commanded the *City of South Haven* and the *Eastland*.

Frank Schwimm of Michigan City and Samuel Olebsky of Chicago served as firemen. Coal passer E. L. Weaver of Dowagiac, Michigan, worked with another man whose name was not recorded. Oiler Frank Kelly was from Alpena, Michigan; his relief was George Brown of Chicago. Chef Max Sanders and second cook Charles Warner were also both from Chicago. Rounding out the crew was young purser James Anderson, only twenty-three years old. On such a voyage the *Soo City* certainly did not need a purser, but Anderson, who once served in a similar capacity on the steamer *Saugatuck*, was given the opportunity of making the "once in a lifetime" trip, doing whatever he could to make himself useful. He accepted with pleasure.

Anderson was from the village of Montague, Michigan, and was engaged to marry a neighborhood girl, Miss Grace Baxter.[2] They had tentatively set the wedding date for some time after he returned from New Orleans. Before bidding goodby to Miss Baxter, his mother, and younger brother, Adolph,[3] James promised to send the editor of the Montague *Observer* news of the vessel's progress and his own impressions of distant and thrilling scenes few of Montague's citizens would ever enjoy.

It took the *Soo City* eleven days to wend her way around the "thumb" of Michigan, sail down the St. Clair and Detroit rivers, steam the length of Lake Erie, transit the Wel-

[2] Grace Baxter eventually married Grant Johnston, who later became chief engineer of the *City of Muskegon* of the Crosby Line. He was serving in that capacity when the vessel crashed into the south pier at Muskegon, in an early morning gale in October of 1919. Seven of the crew and more than twenty of the thirty-seven passengers, most of whom were asleep, perished. One of the victims was Johnston's mother, Kate.

[3] James Anderson's brother, Adolph, eighteen at the time, later became a Montague banker and member of the board of directors of the Hackley Union National Bank & Trust Company.

land Canal, and make the long haul down Lake Ontario to Cape Vincent and the St. Lawrence River. Fifty-nine miles down the river she docked at Ogdensburg, New York, where she was scheduled to take on coal bunkers and sign on four more crew members. Here, too, Captain Dority, at the geographical limit of his freshwater license, would surrender command to Captain John G. Dillon, former skipper of the government transport vessel *Missouri*. Captain Dillon had an unlimited saltwater ticket and much previous experience along unfriendly coasts where tides and currents raced and fall storms were frequent. It was, obviously, a temporary assignment, for Captain Dillon had assured his wife and three small children that he would return to their Brooklyn, New York, home in a matter of a week or ten days.

While the *Soo City* hunkered under Hall's derrick to load her coal bunkers, word went out that a few berths were available. Chief engineer Warwick wanted to sign on two more firemen. The local agent of the Firemen's Union, Mr. Smith, sent him two men, Joe Ceazer and Joe Sovie. Alexander McLain signed on as an able seaman, and nineteen-year-old Peter Gauthier came aboard as a wheelsman.

Bunkers full and additional galley supplies loaded, the *Soo City* departed Ogdensburg on November eleventh, but with only three of the new men aboard. At the last moment, when he learned that return-trip fare home was not included in the deal, fireman Sovie stamped off the vessel in a fit of pique.

James Anderson, in his first dispatch to the Montague *Observer,* proved enthralled by the scenic Thousand Islands, the bucolic vistas along the Lachine Canal, and the distant blue mountains. But he took a dim view of Montreal, which he found dirty, muddy, and very old-fashioned, inhabited mostly by French. However, he grew positively poetic at the sight of Quebec, its towering bastions, the Liverpool liners at the docks, and a British man-of-war moored nearby, concluding:

> . . . Here I must say good-bye as our pilot leaving us has promised to take this ashore to mail. Hoping this has been of some interest to you and promising a bit more in regards to this trip, I am,
>
> Very sincerely yours
> Jas. Anderson

Outbound from Quebec beyond the Saguenay River and in the broadening St. Lawrence, the people of the *Soo City*, or at least those who had sailed from Michigan City, got their first taste of saltwater spray, saw whales lazily surfacing and spouting, and developed a second set of "sea legs" as the steamer adjusted to a new environment of much longer sea crests and lifting, rolling swells.

Young James Anderson must have been enraptured at the sight of many steamers slogging in from the Atlantic, salt-rimed and heavy with cargo for Montreal and Quebec. Little ports along the river also had their own types of vessels designed for the local pulp wood and fishing trade, all with hulls of red, blue, bright green, and white. Always there were the towering mountains on both sides, with a dozen shades of blue and grey vanishing into infinity, with little villages nestled at their feet along the river, each with a church spire reaching high over the clusters of little homes and the ever-present river dock.

The course set for the *Soo City* by Captain Dillon would take her out to where the St. Lawrence became as wide as Lake Michigan itself, before hauling to starboard on the Gaspé Passage course between the picturesque Gaspé Peninsula and the wreck-studded shores of Anticosti Island. Then, still constant, the course would remain steady through the Gulf of St. Lawrence, keeping the Magdalen Islands well off to starboard as the vessel steamed on through Cabot Strait, between Cape Breton Island and Newfoundland. The *Soo City* would then be in the open Atlantic, and her charted voyage would take her off Nova Scotia and onward to Boston and New York.

But the *Soo City* never found the welcome shelter of busy New York harbor. Nor did she put in at any of the ports where a vessel, battered by storm or laboring along and beset with mechanical trouble, could find succor or help. In New York, a full week after the steamer's departure from Quebec, agent Franklin dispatched wires to several ports in the Maritimes, seeking word of the vessel and asking shipping people to keep watch for her. The Maritime Exchange, when she was ten days overdue, officially listed her missing and presumed lost.

Back in Michigan City, W. K. Greenbaum, general manager of the Indiana Transportation Company, was receiving anxious inquiries from the families of the crew. He, too, dashed off wires to authorities at ports where the *Soo City* might possibly have put in for fuel or repairs. But the answers were always the same; no ship answering to that name or description had touched there.

But up off Cape Ray, on the westernmost point of Newfoundland, offshore fishermen discovered what had happened to the *Soo City*. Some days after a great storm, they found the heaving sea littered with timbers. Sloshing along among them were sixty life preservers, all marked "*Soo City*." There were also parts of cabins, hand rails, steamer chairs, furniture, and clothing.

The forty-eight-hour storm that had apparently sent the old passenger and excursion steamer down was of unusual severity, even for an area where monstrous gales and storms had long been part and parcel of every sailor's way of life. It was a breeding ground for nature's gross excesses and had been since the beginning of time. This terrible storm had come raging down from the North Atlantic, steam-rolled through the Strait of Belle Isle and into the Gulf of St. Lawrence, driving before it mountainous seas and bringing intermittent blizzards of stinging snow. No less than ten sturdy fishing vessels from Stephenville and Port aux Barques, on the Newfoundland coast, had been lost, three with all hands.

Again, back in Michigan City, general manager Greenbaum found it difficult to accept the fact that the solid old *Soo City* had surrendered to a storm. He dug out newspaper stories from the happy occasion of her maiden voyage to Sault Ste. Marie. The local paper had adjudged the vessel "solidly and compactly built, diagonally strapped with steel arches inside and out and beneath the deck, which secures a firmness that can be obtained in no other way." Mr. Greenbaum found it inconceivable that she had gone down due to stress of weather. But then Mr. Greenbaum had never been aboard a vessel in the storm-lashed

waters of the Gulf of St. Lawrence. Neither had the newspaper writer who had extolled the vessel's structural
strength.

Previous to Mr. Greenbaum's doubts and laments, but
after James Anderson's first travelogue had been printed
in the Montague *Observer*, there occurred an eerie phenomenon that still defies explanation. At eight o'clock one
dark evening, Adolph Anderson trudged down to the post
office to see if the evening Pere Marquette train from
Muskegon had brought mail from his brother. The post
office gathering was a popular pastime in Montague,
friends and neighbors pausing to exchange pleasantries and
nuggets of news.

Meanwhile, back in the Anderson home on Sheridan
Street,[4] Mrs. Anderson was startled to hear noises upstairs,
familiar noises made by young men racketing about, as
James and Adolph were wont to do. She ventured upstairs
but found everything quiet and in order. Later, on the
evening of December 4th, came the telegram from Mr.
Greenbaum telling of the loss of the *Soo City*. "That was
the noise I heard," said Mrs. Anderson, "just like the boys
racketing about."

Both Adolph Anderson and Mr. Greenbaum carried on
extensive correspondence with seafaring people in the
Maritime Provinces, exploring every possible lead, hoping
that some of the *Soo City*'s people might have survived to
find refuge on one of the remote Magdalen Islands.

On January 4, 1909, Mr. Greenbaum forwarded to

4 John A. "Lex" Chisholm, veteran Muskegon newspaperman and writer
of the column "The Chisholm Trail," recalls visiting the Anderson's Sheridan Street home as a boy, on one occasion taking a fancy to a small banjo,
which the Anderson boys gave him.

Adolph a letter received from Captain Ernest Wells, of Halifax, Nova Scotia, master of the mail and supply vessel *Amelia.* Wrote Captain Wells:

I have made my last trip to the Magdalen Islands for the season. I left the island on the twenty-first of December for Halifax and ports of call. If any of your crew escaped in lifeboats and landed on any part of Magdalen Island, Brion Island or Bird Rock or any part of Cape Breton we would have heard of it. There are people settled all over Magdalen Island and mostly all along the seashore. There are three or four families on Brion Island and one family on Bird Rock. The top of that island is about 400 square feet. I do not believe the crew took to lifeboats, thinking that they would have a better chance to stay with the ship. The weather at that time being so very cold and stormy. I have made inquiries up to date but cannot get any information, and I assure you sir, I feel very bad over such a thing happening and all the relatives have my deepest sympathy.

From New York, Mr. Franklin, the *Soo City*'s agent, had also instigated investigation as to possible survivors, pursuing a rumor that they might be on Bird Rock. The Canadian Minister of Marine and Fisheries regretfully scotched this tale in a letter dated January 12, 1909, reporting that inquiries made by his department gave no support to the rumor and pointing out that the lighthouse keeper easily could have signaled Magdalen Island, as there had been several clear days after the storm. "If there was the slightest possibility of finding any of the crew," he wrote, "the Department would gladly assist to the utmost, but the belief that some of them are on Bird Rock may safely be put down to rumor for which there is no foundation."

One wild, implausible hope momentarily sustained those who mourned the *Soo City* and her crew. Near Cape Ray, Newfoundland, where the vessel's life preservers and wreckage had been found, more life preservers—quite a number of them—had been discovered. They bore the name *S. S. Stanley!*

Had there been a collision? Was the *Stanley* an ocean-going vessel that might have picked up survivors only to continue her voyage? Highly unlikely. Investigators quickly pinned down the fact that the only steamer *Stanley* in Canadian waters at the time was a government ice-breaker that was still in port at Charlottetown, Prince Edward Island. Some suggested that the life preservers had been purchased, used, when the *Soo City* was still in the Lake Michigan excursion trade. Possible, but again highly unlikely. This mystery was never solved.

All hope for the men of the *Soo City* had been abandoned by the time the summer freight, passenger, and excursion season came again to Lake Michigan in 1909. Owners still fought vigorously for business, mostly by advertising their vessels as being the fastest, safest, most commodious, and elegantly outfitted craft available. Ironically, these were the same terms applied to the old *Soo City*, back in 1888.

6

·
·
·
·

⚓

The Egg Harbor Express

Any vessel that provides transportation for people and supplies over a period of years, thus furnishing the goods of life and a means of livelihood in remote places, eventually endears herself to those she serves, however mordant their utterances on her behalf.

They may make scornful references as to her speed and appearance, poke fun at her management, and deride her accommodations. Over the long haul, however, she earns a grudging acceptance and a degree of affection simply by coming and going, despite a capricious adherence to schedules and routes. The ship is, after all, the most convenient, sometimes the only, link to friends, relatives, and distant places. They may revile her with sarcastic nicknames, make abrasive comments as to her seaworthiness, and use pungent terms to describe her crew. But in the final analysis she is "their" boat.

The *Erie L. Hackley*, twenty-one years of steady service behind her, was just such a vessel, or at least Captain

Joseph Vorous hoped she would attain that enviable status when he, Henry Robertoy, Orin Rowin, and Edgar Thorp bought her in the spring of 1903 for $3,000.

Captain Vorous thought she would work out nicely for the service he was starting between various Green Bay ports in Wisconsin. It was admittedly a somewhat precarious venture financially, since some time would naturally elapse before the people and small businesses in the communities she planned to serve would accept the *Hackley* as a steady, on-going institution. One of the partners, engineer Orin Rowin, hard pressed for funds, was having his share of the purchase price deducted from his wages at a rate of twenty dollars a month.

Captain Vorous and his partners had no delusions of grandeur. They would ply a simple route that would provide a living for the *Hackley*'s owners and just a little money additional to set aside for a larger vessel should the service generate enough business.

"I don't want to set the world on fire," he confided to friends and associates, "just establish something that will continue on after us."

The route, as initiated, began at Sturgeon Bay. From that point the *Hackley* would steam directly across Green Bay to Menominee. From there she would come back across the bay to Egg Harbor, sixteen miles north of Sturgeon Bay. Then, from Egg Harbor to Fish Creek it was a short voyage, in the lee of the land and protected from unpleasant weather from any direction but directly west and north. From Fish Creek it was almost a straight shot up the Strawberry Channel and past Eagle Bluff until it was time to haul to starboard on the course to Detroit Harbor, on Washington Island.

Intermediate stops could be made, if freight or passengers offered, at Sister Bay or Ellison Bay. What's more, the route afforded several harbors of refuge should weather conditions dictate. Shanty Bay, behind Horseshoe Island; Eagle Harbor; and Hedgehog Harbor, protected by Deathdoor Bluff, offered sufficient water and good holding ground.

But in six months the *Hackley* had earned only one nickname, the "Egg Harbor Express." It was probably an expression of frustration by the residents of Egg Harbor because they arrived home, after departing Sturgeon Bay, only after a thirty-two-mile round trip across Green Bay to Menominee.

Captain Vorous was from Fish Creek, and the *Hackley* crew quickly took on a "hometown" look. In addition to partner Henry Robertoy, cook Carl Pelkey, deckhand Freeman Thorp, fireman Blaine McSweeney, purser Frank Blakefield, and engineer Orin Rowin were "Fish Creekers," as they were known. The single exception was deckhand Hugh Miller, who hailed from Charlevoix, Michigan. Appropriately, the service began under the official name of Fish Creek Transportation Company.

Green Bay is a large body of water contiguous to Lake Michigan. Anywhere but in the Great Lakes country it would qualify as a lake in its own right. The surrounding countryside at the turn of the century, on both the Wisconsin mainland and the Door County Peninsula, was rugged with primitive roads. The most convenient access to shoreside communities was still by boat.

Other steamers served the larger, more accessible ports, but Captain Vorous was of the opinion that the modest size of the *Hackley* would enable him to build up a steady trade where docks and depths of water were limiting factors. The *Hackley*, built in Muskegon, Michigan, in 1882, was 79 feet long, slightly over 17 feet in beam, and drew only a little over 5 feet of water. Her steam plant, although modest, was considered adequate and had served her well.

At 11:00 A.M. on Saturday, October 3, 1903, the *Hackley* left Sturgeon Bay, bound across Green Bay to Menominee with about her normal complement of passengers but with a larger-than-usual cargo of general freight, from barrels of beer to bolts of cloth.

The wind had been blowing steadily from the south-southwest all night, and a considerable sea was running. But Captain Vorous did not consider waiting for better weather. The *Hackley*, encountering quartering seas all the way, made her way safely over the sixteen-mile course to Menominee, although it must have been a memorable voyage for some of the passengers.

At Menominee a few passengers departed and others came aboard. Some additional freight was also loaded and stowed while Captain Vorous availed himself of the latest weather report. Under ominous, leaden skies, a somewhat diminished southwest wind and sea still prevailed. Oddly, the weather report predicted a sudden shift of wind to northwest before long, with heavy squalls.

The *Hackley* left Menominee at about 5:45 P.M., shortly after Captain Vorous confided to purser Blakefield that he thought they could make it safely back across the bay to Egg Harbor before the squall struck.

Drawing by Dick Dugan

The *Erie L. Hackley* was called many things after she foundered. Before that she was known to many as the "Egg Harbor Express."

Significantly, Ed Thorp, one of her owners, had intended returning home to Fish Creek on the *Hackley*, but, after viewing the skies, seas, and flying gale warnings, he had a sudden change of mind. Perhaps mental telepathy was a factor in his decision, for only the night before, his brother, Roy, had a terrible dream in which he envisioned the *Hackley* battling a great storm on Green Bay before the little steamer gave a sudden lurch and went down. So vivid was the dream that on Saturday Roy considered telephoning Menominee to ask Ed not to make the trip. But, fearing that his dream would be laughed at, he did not make the call.

Fifteen minutes out of Menominee, with the *Hackley* plugging along on the Egg Harbor course and laboring under seas attacking her starboard stern counter, purser Blakefield noticed that Captain Vorous had the pilot house door open on the port side and was anxiously scanning the skies to the northwest, from which direction the squall was predicted to strike. Indeed, the skies in that quadrant gave every evidence of incipient trouble: low, dark, and turbulent clouds that usually spawn tempests of winds and seas.

The squall did materialize as predicted. But unaccountably, diabolically, it came from the same, prevailing, southwest direction. Building up for hundreds of miles, it hit with a stunning, paralyzing force, pushing monstrous seas before it, rearing big graybeards that smashed into the *Hackley* with such savagery that she instantly heeled sharply and dangerously to port, hammered over on her beam ends.

Captain Vorous, desperately attempting to right his vessel, turned her wheel hard to port to bring her head around and into the wind and seas. But in the maneuver the *Hackley* got only part way around and then fell off into the trough of the seas. Although the engine was laboring at maximum power, the ship simply would not come around. She just stayed there like a floating log as the seas climbed aboard.

Purser Blakefield ran to the pilot house to help the captain turn the steamer to starboard, where she could run before the seas. It was his feeling that if Captain Vorous succeeded in turning to port and getting the *Hackley* facing the wind and seas, he would try to find shelter in the lee of Green Island, a mile south of the steamer's course.

Once down in the troughs of the seas, the first comber to assail her from starboard smashed in the solid gangway shutters on the lower or freight deck, allowing several tons of water to enter the hull, heeling her down dramatically to starboard. Succeeding seas then poured in the gangways and over her open stern counter.

In two minutes the *Hackley* was gone, going down by the stern in a great compression of air that blew off part of her lower deck and all of the upper deck and cabins. So rudely had the passengers and crew been buffeted about during the *Hackley*'s short combat with the seas that not one managed to grab a life preserver, although there were plenty aboard.

In the horrifying first moments after the steamer went down, crewmen and passengers were tossed about in the floating wreckage, most of them grasping at anything that would support their weight. But the wreckage itself, assaulted by the big, breaking seas, disintegrated rapidly. The only section that remained relatively intact was part of the upper deck, and most of the few who survived found support there. While their combined weight kept the deck submerged most of the time, the railings were still above water and provided a place to hang on.

Eleven people, including Captain Vorous, perished almost immediately. Eight others clung to wreckage throughout the cold and turbulent night. Purser Blakefield fashioned a small raft from two timbers and managed to survive. Under different circumstances he might have been amused at the early morning sight of the *Hackley*'s pilot house rolling like a barrel in the seas, the steering wheel intact, and the captain's coat still swinging from a hook.

The survivors were still there, all eight of them, late the next morning when they were spotted from the steamer *Sheboygan*. Captain Asa Johnson of the *Sheboygan* had wisely holed up at Washington Harbor during the storm. Had he kept to his original schedule, his vessel would undoubtedly have steamed past the numbed survivors in the dark of the night.

It was Thomas Nelson, a passenger of the *Sheboygan*, who first spotted the wreckage and reported it to the second mate. The officer maintained that what Nelson saw was merely floating logs. But Nelson insisted that it was wreckage and that he could see a man on it. The captain was summoned and with the aid of his glasses confirmed Nelson's sighting.

In marine-oriented communities, where ships and the men who sail or take passage on them are friends and neighbors, indignation runs high when a vessel and her people are lost. It is particularly strong and bitter when a skipper's judgment and the seaworthiness of his command are questioned. In the case of Captain Joseph Vorous, both owner and skipper, he was doubly damned.

Always, too, there are whispered tales, reports, rumors, and idle yarns, most of them seeming to point out strange coincidences and premonitions.

Roy Thorp's dream was one of them. So was his brother Ed's last-minute decision not to sail on the boat. Another story making the rounds was that Grace Vorous, the captain's sister, had planned to return to Fish Creek on the *Hackley* but had been advised not to by the captain because of the threatening weather. (Actually, Grace was in the Menominee hospital at the time and was not planning to return home until the following Thursday.)

One tale had it that the steamer's boiler was in poor order—had, indeed, been condemned by government inspectors.

Gossip had it, too, that purser Blakefield had one thousand dollars in his pockets when the vessel went down, but was asserting that all the ship's money went down with her. Blakefield pointed out that the *Hackley* did not earn that kind of money and that, instead of one thousand dollars in the till, less than one hundred dollars was involved, and it was in his desk drawer at the time of the steamer's loss, not in his pockets.

Ed Thorp, understandably wishing that brother Roy had never mentioned his dream, insisted that his decision had nothing to do with the seaworthiness of the *Hackley*.

"I was of a mind to make the trip," he maintained, "but when I saw the weather conditions, being a poor sailor, I was of a mind not to."

And engineer Orin Rowin scotched the defective boiler rumor by pointing out that it had been inspected and found in good order and a certificate to that effect was in the company office.

Nasty early rumors suggested that Captain Vorous was somewhat inclined to the juice of the grape. His father, Levi Vorous, enraged by the gossip, stated flatly that his son was a competent navigator who neither drank liquor nor used tobacco in any form. Others close to the family verified this statement.

In Sturgeon Bay, the *Advocate*, [1] a unique newspaper founded by pioneer publisher Joseph Harris in 1862, was conscious of all the unfounded gossip and sought to keep things in perspective, printing the contradictions as new rumors circulated, including the indignant reaction of Levi Vorous.

Unfortunately, the *Hackley* had not been around long enough to earn the affection and tolerance Captain Vorous had hoped would eventually be her reward. Consequently, both he and the *Hackley* came in for heavy fire from critics, ashore and afloat.

Some were quick to point out that the freight deck had no scuppers, or not enough, to drain off the uninvited seas that came romping aboard in boisterous weather conditions, and that successive seas piling in through the broken gangways or over the open stern would inevitably eventually drive her down. But others were mindful of the fact that the *Hackley*, in substantially the same passenger and freight business, had sailed for twenty years on the Manitou Island service on lower Lake Michigan, a vastly more exposed course as compared to her Green Bay route. Yet she had managed to survive nicely.

The marine men were somewhat in agreement, however, in faulting the judgment of the captain when he attempted to turn the *Hackley* to port into the wind and seas. With the propeller or "wheel" of the vessel turning to the right, as most did, the vessel thus capable of responding faster on a right or starboard turn, a turn to starboard would have given the advantage of slight additional speed

---

[1] The *Advocate*, founded by Joseph Harris, is now the *Door County Advocate*, published by the founder's great grandson, Chandler Harris.

and momentum, which might possibly have gotten the *Hackley* around. But this was a tenuous, theoretical conclusion.

In due time, but with sentiment still high, the official government inspectors came to Sturgeon Bay to investigate the disaster and delineate the probable causes. Inspector General George Uhler and Supervising Inspector Wescott subpoenaed Wallace Hill, Roy Thorp, and purser Frank Blakefield, all of whom had intimate knowledge of the *Hackley* and her condition. Also testifying were William Rieboldt, Sam Johnson, and Charles Armstrong, caulkers at the local shipyard at the time of the *Hackley*'s last overhaul.

Captain William Morris, owner and master of the schooner *Lydia*, earlier volunteered his opinion that the *Hackley* was quite safe and that ten years earlier he had assisted in giving her a thorough rebuild.

"When we got done, she was as good as new," said Captain Morris.

He also commented that on the evening the *Hackley* surrendered to the elements, the *Lydia* had been at dock in Sturgeon Bay with a full cargo and deck load of lumber. At about the time of the disaster, he reported, the storm generated brief periods of wind so fierce that the top layers of lumber had been blown around the dock area like jackstraws.

The inspectors departed with their transcribed testimony, notes, and depositions and in due time rendered their verdict. It was their conclusion that the *Hackley* was in a seaworthy state when she left Menominee, since she had crossed Green Bay many times under weather conditions such as existed at the time of her departure, and always without incident. Nor, they ruled, could Captain Vorous have foretold that the squall would come from an entirely different direction than predicted. It was further concluded that the steamer had been caught in the vortex of hurricane-force winds that, because of the *Hackley*'s relatively high superstructure, were a contributing factor in "pushing her down" while in the trough of the seas, thus preventing her completion of her attempted turn.

In short, the loss of the *Hackley* was attributed entirely to something man is powerless to control: "stress of weather."

Captain Vorous had been prophetic about the potential of the new steamer service when it began, the "Egg Harbor Express" did not set the world on fire.

7

⚓

"... Perhaps More Honored in the Breach"

Things were tough in 1936. The Great Depression, a malignant scourge that had stalked the world economy for six years, had seemingly sapped the life from nations and their peoples. Nowhere were the dread manifestations more pronounced than in the shipping industry. Saltwater ports were crowded with skilled seamen now "on the beach," while at dockside or tethered to mooring buoys in the roadsteads of the world, hundreds of freighters grew scabrous with rust and neglect.

On the Great Lakes many of the long steamers were idle, anchored in clusters in protected waterways or strung out along silent docks, their crews dispersed to join the lines of the unemployed. The few iron ore, coal, and grain carriers that did operate often did so briefly or sporadically. Such were the times that skippers were sailing as wheelsmen, deckhands, and watchmen. Down below, chief engineers worked as second or third engineers, while the former seconds and thirds served as oilers and wipers.

Particularly hard hit were Canada's Maritime Provinces, heavily dependent upon the sea and where jobs, even in good times, were hard to find. From St. John's, Corner Brook, and scores of little granite-rimmed Newfoundland harbors, countless hard-working "Newfies" ranged far afield, restlessly combing the coasts and inlets for jobs. So did their seafaring brethren from New Brunswick and Nova Scotia. Strangely, many found jobs on the Great Lakes, where every port and hiring hall had long lists of qualified but unemployed sailors. One can only suspect that it was because they worked cheaper and demanded less in the way of creature comforts aboard ship.

Nowhere does the jungle telegraph work more effectively than in the world of the sailor. Call it nepotism or what you will, when openings developed or were even rumored, relatives, friends, and neighbors were the first to know and respond. The old adage "a word to the wise" functioned perfectly. Consequently, the crew lists of many Canadian lake vessels found small, deepwater communities heavily represented by seamen working in a variety of capacities.

A case in point was the sandsucker *Sand Merchant* the day she steamed westward from Montreal. It chanced to be June 20, 1936. It was really quite a strange affair, although her owners, the National Sand and Materials Company of Toronto, undoubtedly knew what they were doing. The *Sand Merchant*, after working the coastal trade, was ordered to rendezvous with another company sandsucker, the *Charles Dick*, Captain Graham McLelland master, at Montreal. Here the *Sand Merchant*'s crew was paid off and the

Charles Dick's men transferred to her. The *Charles Dick*, presumably, would later muster another crew and replace the *Sand Merchant* in the company's coastal areas of operation. The *Sand Merchant* would go to the lower lakes, there to bustle about her business of sucking up several grades of sand from the bottom of Lake Erie, delivering it to various ports. She would range about a bit because the sand was used primarily in the construction and building trades, which, like everything else, were vastly depressed.

There was a curious mixture of friends and relatives aboard the *Sand Merchant* when she departed Montreal. Together they comprised more than half of her crew of twenty-six. Captain McLelland was from Cape Tormentine, New Brunswick, as was fireman Harold Cannon. From the nearby New Brunswick communities of New Castle, Rexton, and Bay du Vin Beach were William Gifford, Roland DeMille, Peter Daigle, John Hebert, and Walter McGinness, the vessel's chief engineer. From Cape Breton, Nova Scotia, came second engineer Martin White and his son, Harry, a deckhand. Other Nova Scotia men were deck engineer Jack Meuse, from Yarmouth, and Nicholas McCarthy, an oiler.

But the largest representation was not from the Maritime Provinces but from Victoria Harbor, Ontario, in the heart of the Georgian Bay country. Second mate Daniel Bourrie must have had influence somewhere, for shipmates were his brother, Wilfred, a wheelsman; Alphonse Robitaille, his brother-in-law from nearby Midland; and the three Dault brothers, Herman, Joseph, and Amos. Also from Victoria Harbor was Sanford Gray, third engineer.

Herman Dault was the only member of the original paid-off crew of the *Sand Merchant* to get hired back on. Although he had a mate's certificate, he had been working as a wheelsman and now was happy to accept a job as crane operator.

First and second cooks Henry Lytle and Frank Burns, both from Toronto, had been working together for years. First mate Bernie Drinkwater was from Port Stanley, and the rest were from scattered communities along the lakes, from Thorold to Ft. William, Ontario.

En route to her Lake Erie assignment the *Sand Merchant* took on a load of sand in Lake Ontario near Simcoe Island, delivered it to Toronto, and made a single trip from Niagara to Toronto before Captain McLelland, now in his third year as a skipper, took his vessel through the Welland Canal and into Lake Erie.

The primary Lake Erie pumping grounds for the sandsuckers was off the Canadian shore, between Southeast Shoal Light and Point Pelee, near the western basin of the lake.

Like the *Charles Dick*, the *Sand Merchant* was specially designed and built at the Collingwood Shipyards as a self-loader and unloader. Large port and starboard suction pipes were lowered into the sand banks on the bottom. Large centrifugal pumps sucked the sand aboard and propelled the mixture of sand and water along pipes or ducts on each side of the vessel, passing through screens and into the two hopper-like cargo holds. The excess water coming inboard was drained from the sand cargo by spillways provided for that purpose, through the vessel's sides. Water that escaped the spillways found its way to a sump in the after-ends of the hoppers and was discharged overboard by a special pump.

The *Sand Merchant* did not have hatch covers over the open cargo hoppers, this made possible by her unusual supplementary buoyancy features, four particularly large tanks fitted on either side of the cargo hoppers. These buoyancy reserves were in addition to her usual tank capacity. The ship was, in other words, designed to be a stable, seaworthy vessel despite the temporary fluidity of her cargo, which quickly settled down into a dense, inert mass. The hatch or hopper coamings themselves extended thirty inches above the deck, and no amount of water coming aboard during stress of weather conditions should alter her stability to a significant degree. Topsides she was a rather strange-looking creation by virtue of the framework that supported her unloading boom and the continuous conveyor belt and buckets that dug out the cargo. Cranes forward, lowered, raised, and maneuvered the long suction pipes. Baroque in appearance, the *Sand Merchant* was the epitome of efficiency, built to do a specific job with a minimum of blustering or complaining.

Once on Lake Erie she went about her workaday tasks with the ship, master, and crew evolving a methodical routine that varied little except for cargo destinations. The construction business being at a low ebb, the *Sand Merchant* wandered about a bit, sucking up sand east of Pelee Point and delivering her loads to Marysville and Port Huron, along the St. Clair River, and to Windsor, Cleveland, Toledo, and Lorain. When both hoppers were up to their usual marks with cargo, the total burden was about 2200 cubic yards (2900 tons). When fully laden the ship slogged along at a sedate pace of about eight and one-half miles per hour.

At nine o'clock on the evening of Friday, October 16, 1936, shortly after unloading a cargo of sand at Windsor, Ontario, the *Sand Merchant* departed her dock for the five and one-half hour trip back to the pumping grounds. Missing from the crew roster was boatswain John Hebert, of Rexton, New Brunswick, who had received permission to lay off for one trip. But the total complement of people aboard remained the same, since first mate Bernie Drinkwater had arranged for his wife, Lillian, to make a trip. The *Sand Merchant*'s next cargo was to be delivered to Cleveland, after which another load was scheduled for Windsor, where Mrs. Drinkwater would depart. It was against the rules, of course, but the life of a sailor is a lonely one, and skippers were often wont to wink at official dictums.

At approximately 2:30 A.M. on the seventeenth, the *Sand Merchant* arrived at her designated working area. The large suction pipes were lowered and the process of taking aboard another cargo began. It was a clamorous operation, with the big pumps thundering and water and sand surging through the pipes, along with the clanging and other noises associated with a working vessel. It was a din that off-duty seamen learned to live with and ignore.

At two o'clock on Saturday afternoon, the hoppers having received their normal capacity, the suction pipes were raised and the *Sand Merchant* came around on the Cleveland course. The wind was blowing quite briskly from the northwest, lifting a modest sea and tearing the black smoke from the boat's funnel, driving it on ahead in fragmented streamers.

The vessel had been under way for less than an hour when her steering cable parted. Captain McLelland immediately ordered the port anchor dropped, and when the sandsucker had been brought around, head to wind and sea, the task of renewing the broken cable began. This required removing two oval manhole covers on the starboard side of the deck so men could enter the buoyancy tanks to pass the new cable through each bulkhead. Herman and Amos Dault were included in the repair gang, and when the job was completed Herman personally supervised the bolting down of the manhole covers or scuppers. At six o'clock the anchor was hoisted and the voyage to Cleveland was resumed.

Tired, Captain McLelland had his dinner and then lay down to nap on a settee in the rear of the wheelhouse, instructing second mate Bourrie to call him when the vessel neared the Cleveland water intake "crib," five miles off the harbor entrance.

Meanwhile, the northwest wind had increased in force and sloppy following seas began boarding the *Sand Merchant* with some regularity. Captain McLelland was not a man who worried much about weather, although other shipmasters on Lake Erie that night were inclined to do so. Shortly after the steering cable repairs had been completed and the *Sand Merchant* put on her Cleveland course, two other vessels, the *George L. Eaton* and the *Prescott*, cleared Pelee Passage, eastbound. Their masters, not liking the look of things, both hauled to port, taking the north shore route down Lake Erie, where both craft, each of which had much more freeboard than the *Sand Merchant*, would be in the lee of the land, in much calmer seas.

Two hours after he had put his head down for a nap Captain McLelland was awakened by the second mate, who advised him that the steamer had taken on a list to port. The list was not severe but seemed to be increasing steadily and for no apparent reason.

Captain McLelland did the only thing that made sense under the existing conditions, which included freshening winds and higher seas: he hauled the *Sand Merchant* around, checked down to half speed ahead, and took the wheel himself while his men sought out the reason for the list. In the half-ahead engine status, practically hove-to, he noted that the vessel was getting sluggish, a fact he later attributed to seas roaming over the open hatches, carrying sand and water into the "wings" or open spaces under the deck, along the hoppers or holds. When his rudder manipulations and more speed on the engine failed to keep the *Sand Merchant* headed into the wind and seas, the vessel growing more sluggish with every passing moment, the good Captain McLelland concluded that foundering was not only a possibility, it was imminent. He had been called by the second mate at about nine o'clock and within a half hour the situation had become hopeless. On the assumption that through some mishap or mistake the large buoyancy tanks on the port side had been damaged and thus open to the sea, the crew had operated the associated pumps but got no water. If there was a leak, and obviously there was a catastrophic one, it was not in the buoyancy tank. Other compartments, the pump room, and machinery spaces were likewise clear of inrushing waters. Still, the list increased by the moment.

Shortly after he had been awakened Captain Mc-Lelland had ordered his mates, Drinkwater and Bourie, to prepare the lifeboats for launching. Bourrie secured the flares from the lifeboats and proceeded to fire them off. The ship's whistle began sounding the distress signal, and some of the crew augmented the flares by burning mattresses and bedding on the boat deck. It was a macabre situation and so incongruous—a vessel sinking literally within sight of the lights of Cleveland, displaying and sounding the age-old signals of distress for the better part of an hour and yet going down apparently without a soul ashore or afloat being aware of her plight.[1]

[1] When no help arrived in response to their flares and numerous mattresses set ablaze, the crew of the *Sand Merchant* could only conclude that their desperate signals went unobserved. As a matter of fact they were seen, but by people who did not interpret their meaning.

After three weeks of fruitless searching for the wreck, U.S. Corps of Engineers people made a survey of shoreline residents west of Cleveland, seeking citizens who may have sighted anything unusual on the lake the night of October seventeenth.

Bert Morrison, a compass adjuster, had already reported that on the night of the disaster, as he drove into the yard of his home, he had noticed a vessel's running lights. As he saw no distress signals at the time, he concluded that it was a ship swinging around at anchor or a fishing tug delayed in its work.

Still seeking witnesses, K. M. Harvey of the Corps of Engineers later talked to August Vian, who operated a barbecue restaurant just east of Lorain. He had not noticed any flares but had observed the fitful blazing of the mattresses, a sight he did not associate with a vessel in distress.

Another witness was Geraldine Kotz of Avon Lake. Returning home after a school meeting shortly before ten o'clock that fateful night, she watched some unusual light aboard a vessel. Since the rest of her family were already in bed, she made no mention of it until the next morning, when she remarked that someone on the boat must have been holding a Fourth of July celebration.

Later, by plotting Mrs. Kotz's estimated line of sight with those of August Vian and Bert Morrison, Captain Nimrod Long took the government steamer *Peary* to the triangular spot on the chart where the lines of

Although first mate Bernie Drinkwater aroused the off-duty hands and urged them topsides, he remained strangely missing from the boat deck, where his shipboard responsibilities required that he take charge of preparing and launching the lifeboats. Second mate Bourrie took over in the emergency. Mate Drinkwater was witnessed several times near the door of his room, on the starboard side, forward, apparently trying to calm his distraught wife.

It was an eerie scene there on the boat deck as crewmen tried to lower the boats. Only slight illumination was provided by a couple of feeble light bulbs and the burning mattresses, which flared up occasionally and smoked villainously. Due to the pronounced list to port the starboard boat could not be launched, so the falls were slashed to permit it to float free when the steamer went down. The port boat was lowered even with the canting deck, and some of the crew climbed aboard while others operated the falls. Sometime during the nightmarish scrambling in the dark, first mate Drinkwater must have come up on the boat deck, for when deck engineer Jack Meuse saw the port lifeboat being lowered, Lillian Drinkwater was aboard.

At this moment the *Sand Merchant* lurched sharply and then, as her coal bunkers shifted, rolled over, disappearing in a cloud of black smoke and steam and with a thunderous noise of conveyors, deck machinery, and unloading gear tearing free. The men had expected her to go soon, but not that suddenly. Captain McLelland, the only man left in the wheelhouse, simply dove free off the bridge wing. Aft, those on the boat deck were thrown clear as the sandsucker

---

sighting converged and there found the *Sand Merchant*, six miles north-northeast of Avon Point.

made her precipitous and fatal roll to port. The port life-boat, still connected to the boat falls, flipped over but broke free. In the space of a few seconds the ship's full comple-ment of crew was thrashing around in the darkness, yell-ing, cursing, and desperately seeking support. Both life-boats surfaced upside down and immediately became ha-vens of refuge for frightened sailors. Mrs. Drinkwater was not among those who gained the temporary security of either boat. Nor did her husband, mate Bernie Drink-water.

Clawing and clutching, but helping one another when they could, nine men found themselves trying to maintain a grip on one boat . . . second cook Frank Burns, John Ider-son, wheelsman Wilfred Bourrie, second mate Daniel Bour-rie, Captain McLelland, fireman Ray Harper, and the brothers Dault—Amos, Joe, and Herman.

The second boat was a frigid haven for Jack Meuse, Harold Cannon, Peter Daigle, second engineer Martin White, William Gifford, and Fred Morse. Both lifeboats were swept repeatedly by the seas, washing the seamen off time and again. Gradually, as cold and exhaustion took their toll, fewer were able to regain their tenuous holds on the keels and rope hand grips. Harold Cannon, Cap-tain McLelland's fellow townsman from Cape Tormentine, was the first to go.

At approximately 8:30 the next morning, Sunday, Oc-tober 18th, two vessel skippers, outbound from Cleveland, were somewhat startled to sight capsized lifeboats bobbing about in the morning slop, each supporting men who waved and shouted. The *Marquette & Bessemer No. 1* maneuvered close to one lifeboat, threw ropes, and hauled in Jack Meuse, Martin White, Fred Morse, and William Gifford. Not far away, the *Thunder Bay Quarries* turned to provide a lee and picked up three men, all that were left from the nine that had clung so tenaciously to their lifeboat throughout the night. They were Captain McLelland, John Iderson, and Herman Dault. Joe Dault had slipped away even as the *Thunder Bay Quarries* turned from her course to effect the rescue.

On both rescue vessels the chilled survivors were hustled into dry clothing and provided with hot food and potent spirits. Their recovery was amazingly rapid. The *Marquette & Bessemer No. 1* retraced her track and delivered the shipwrecked sailors she carried to a Cleveland dock. The *Thunder Bay Quarries,* en route to nearby Sandusky for a coal cargo, continued on to that port, where Captain McLelland and his two crewmen departed in good order.

Ten days later, in the Toronto office of Captain Henry King, Examiner of Masters and Mates, the preliminary inquiry into the foundering of the *Sand Merchant* brought some embarrassing moments and questions for Captain McLelland. There would have been even more embarrassing questions for first mate Drinkwater, but, alas, he was beyond this life.

Captain King, a kindly man, merely sought to determine if the master of the *Sand Merchant* had been conscientious in his handling of his vessel and his men.

Q. When you got underway after the transmission cable repairs had been completed, about six o'clock, what course were you on?

A. Sou'east by east.

Q. Was that magnetic or by compass?

Photo from the Milton J. Brown collection

Not a thing of beauty, but a sturdy, utilitarian vessel, the *Margaret Olwill* was photographed just before she began loading cargo for her last, fateful trip. Captain and Mrs. Brown are shown standing aft, just forward of the after cabin.

Western Reserve Historical Society photo

Shown here the day it was completed, the bridge was the first such iron structure of the Howe-Truss design.

Philip P. Bliss

BELOW
Wreckage of the bridge and the *Pacific Express* lay intermingled under the supporting piers the day after the disaster.

Western Reserve Historical Society photo

Mass burial site for unidentified victims of the Ashtabula train disaster, marked by this obelisk in the city's Chestnut Grove Cemetery.

After a long career on the Great Lakes, the sturdy passenger and excursion steamer *Soo City* vanished off Newfoundland.

Photo courtesy Marine Historical Collection, Milwaukee Public Library

Lacking many aesthetic maritime features, the *Sand Merchant* just plugged along, performing her workaday chores with efficiency.

Plucked from his perch on the overturned lifeboat of the *Sand Merchant,* a crewman is helped up a ladder by crewmen of the *Thunder Bay Quarries.*

Telling how it happened. Captain Graham McLelland, right, of the ill-fated *Sand Merchant,* relates his tale of shipwreck to Captain James Healey of the rescue steamer *Thunder Bay Quarries.*

Thoroughly encased in ice, the *City of Bangor,* with deck cargo of new automobiles, lies stranded on the tip of Keweenaw Point.

Photo from the Robert I. Schellig, Jr., collection

Chopping out and de-icing the Chrysler automobiles from the deck of the stranded *City of Bangor*.

Photo courtesy of Mrs. Merle Gerred

Used car lot? No, just Charley Maki's barnyard, where the salvaged automobiles found temporary haven while road crews were carving out a path to Calumet, Michigan.

Pride of the lakes when she was launched, the *Superior City* is shown here on her maiden voyage.

Flames light the Buffalo waterfront after the collision. The flaming bow of the *Penobscot,* right, is where her captain and wheelsman died. Beyond the steamer can be seen the flames from the burning *Morania* and *Dauntless.*

Completely gutted by fire, the tug *Dauntless* is still afloat the morning after the collision and explosion.

Interior of the flame-swept pilot house of the *Penobscot,* where Captain Guyette and wheelsman Richardson perished at their posts.

A. Magnetic.

Q. Sou'east by east?

A. Yes.

Q. Are you sure of that? It was sou'east by east, by your compass?

A. Yes.

Q. Then your compass was out. But that of course had no bearing on your sinking.

A. No.

Q. Did you know the deviation of your compass?

A. The one in the wheelhouse . . . you could not go very much by it.

Q. You had a standard compass?

A. Yes.

Q. And it was fairly reliable?

A. Yes.

Q. Did you ever have to have it adjusted?

A. No, I did not get it adjusted; not since I have been on her.

Q. Did you ever have a lifeboat drill on that ship?

A. No, not since I was on her.

Q. The men had not the faintest idea then, how to lower a boat?

A. (No audible answer.)

Q. Do you not think it would have been better if you had a drill once in a while, to let them know exactly where they ought to go, or what they ought to do in case of emergency?

A. (No audible answer.)

Q. And you saw no reason to expect that there was going to be any kind of weather which would bother you when

you left Southeast Shoal, because it would have been the
simplest thing in the world to have slipped over to the
north shore, if you were expecting heavy weather, and
anchored there?

A. Yes.

Q. You felt satisfied there was not going to be anything
there to bother you; is that the idea?

A. That is the idea. I felt sure I could make the trip.

Q. It is too bad; it cost nineteen lives somewhere, and we
must try and find out just what the reason was.

A. (No audible reply.)

Q. Now, as far as the barometer is concerned; what you
saw of it gave you no inkling of any kind of bad weather?

A. No.

Q. 29:90 . . .

A. The barometer which was in the wheelhouse runs
about 27:00 all the time.

Q. That certainly was not right. If that was 27:00 the
bottom would have fallen out of everything.

A. She had been that way all summer.

Q. They were not working?

A. No.

Q. They were out of order?

A. Yes.

Q. Both of them must have been out of order?

A. (No audible answer.)

In the full report of the subsequent three-day investigation of the disaster, Captain McLelland really did not fare
too badly. He was exonerated from blame in the circumstances but open to censure for failing to have lifeboat

drills aboard his vessel and for permitting an unauthorized person to be aboard. Mate Drinkwater, had he been present, would not have gotten off as easily. Mates Drinkwater and Bourrie, particularly Drinkwater, were charged with the responsibility for the heavy loss of life, Bourrie because he had been tardy in awakening Captain McLelland, and Drinkwater because he had completely failed in his assigned and traditional responsibilities as the ship's first officer.

In Superior Court in Toronto, the Honorable Mr. Justice Errol M. McDougall, wreck commissioner, assisted by Captain George D. Frewer and Mr. L. McMillan, nautical assessors, found that the *Sand Merchant*'s foundering was due to the shifting of her cargo of sand, caused by the incursion of water through her open hoppers and *possibly into her special buoyancy space.*

The fact that the vessel should founder in circumstances she was specifically constructed to weather, continued to puzzle the investigators, particularly after Captain McLelland testified that the *Sand Merchant* had several times actually loaded at the pumping grounds when the seas were mounting her deck. In their Annex to the Report, explaining their conclusions, the Court touched on the riddle several times. "Much anxious consideration has been given to the surprising phenomenon that this vessel should have gone down so suddenly. Her buoyancy space was so great and the capacity of her tanks so considerable that it is astounding to note that she should not have remained afloat for some time after she had turned on her side." The Court thoroughly explored the suggestion that the port buoyancy

tanks may not have been quite dry and, through inadvertence or otherwise, may have been wholly or partially
filled with water, but the evidence seems to negate any
such conclusion. How then, could this vessel have disappeared so rapidly?

In the places where seamen gather to ponder the sinking ships and the loss of shipmates, it was apparent that
something had gone amiss, whether by human error or
mechanical failure. The Court could only surmise and
hint as to such a conclusion, for the men who might otherwise have supplied the answers were forever gone.

Although official criticism was directed at others, and
more specifically at her husband, there was no question in
the opinion of the Court that Lillian Drinkwater's presence
aboard the *Sand Merchant* was a contributing factor in the
heavy toll of lives. The Court pointed out that no authority was obtained from the owners and that the "purely
customary privilege" statement by Captain McLelland was
no justification for her being a passenger. Said the Court,

In the sequel this disregard of a rule, *which is perhaps more
honored in the breach,* may have contributed and, in the
opinion of the Court, did contribute materially to the appalling loss of life which occurred. Distracted by the presence of
his wife aboard, the first officer, who is shown to have been a
competent seaman, in the fact of imminent peril to all aboard,
appears rather to have been more solicitous to his wife than to
his obvious and paramount duty of getting the boats out and
the crew aboard, as he had been directed by the master. How
else can the almost total absence or mention of the first officer
be explained? He was seen by one of the witnesses, some twenty

minutes before the ship went down, standing at his cabin door with his wife. From that time forward, no member of the crew mentions him.

So there it was. A month after the ill-fated *Sand Merchant* found her eternal moorings, poor Lillian Drinkwater, who ventured from Port Stanley to be with her husband for one short trip, became, more or less, the *cause célèbre* in the deaths of her husband and seventeen men she scarcely knew. Her presence aboard was an infraction of a rule or regulation, the violation of which had the tacit approval of many shipmasters. It was a governing principle that even the Court admitted *was perhaps more honored in the breach.*

8

⚓

Bedfellows of Keweenaw

November of 1926 was a particularly vexing month for Great Lakes sailors, shippers, and shoreside personnel. It began and ended with protracted gales and blizzards on the upper lakes that shifted sadistically from northwest to northeast, with but only brief, deceptive interludes of relative calm.

Ashore, with ice building in the slips and connecting waterways and ore freezing in the hopper cars, worried dispatchers and traffic managers gnawed their mustaches and pencils as nearly every daily communique from ship reporters and dock officials recited exceedingly dreary tales of delays and frustrations. Countless steamers, it seemed to them, were loaded but "waiting for weather" at Ashland, Duluth, Superior, Fort William, Michipicoten, and Escanaba. Many others, loaded or light, having begun voyages between gales, encountered more atrocious weather and fled for shelter, slipping into the quiet waters of the Portage, tying up at the Lily Pond, or dropping their hooks in the lee of Isle Royale, Michipicoten Island, the Apostle Islands, and the Manitous.

Upbound and downbound vessels on Lake Superior steamed gratefully behind the sheltering bulk of Whitefish Point, circled monotonously around the Slate Islands, or dropped anchor in Bete Grise Bay, protected by the long hook of the Keweenaw Peninsula.

Locking upbound at the Soo at 4:00 P.M. on November 29th, preceded during the day by the *Lethbridge, Philip Block, Midland Prince, Harry Coulby, Huronic,* and *Leonard Hanna,* Captain William J. Mackin took his *City of Bangor* the length of the upper St. Marys River and nosed into Whitefish Bay.

It was a time of decision. He could go to anchor behind Whitefish Point or proceed on the normal upbound course on Lake Superior as had some of the larger and more powerful steamers that had locked through ahead of him and were now but smoke smudges on the horizon. Some shipmasters had promptly hauled to port to join a half dozen other vessels anchored and snugly waiting it out behind Whitefish Point. In the gloom of dusk, their deck lights strung out like the streets of a village as the smoke from their funnels entwined in the wind to go prowling over Tahquamenon Bay, dispersing grudgingly in the pine forests of Point Iroquois.

How much simpler it would have been had Captain Mackin followed suit. But apparently a momentary lessening of wind speed and moderating seas inspired a personal weather evaluation that indicated to him a lull between gales. Obviously other shipmasters, recognizing the limitations of their vessels, did not agree. And ironically, any one of the sheltered steamers was better prepared to cope with surly Lake Superior than the *City of Bangor.*

Captain Mackin took his command into a wretched, tossing panorama of gray-green seas and scudding, restless clouds. One could surmise that before long there would be many occasions when he would have second thought about not joining the anchored fleet behind Whitefish Point; for it was to be an unfortunate voyage— one that ended with his vessel lost and his crew becoming ill-prepared wilderness hikers. It was altogether a devil's broth of circumstances, and one that created a major headache for Walter P. Chrysler, the rising auto magnate.

The *City of Bangor* was built in 1896 as a conventional straight deck bulk cargo carrier. Along with the almost identical *Penobscot,* she had been purchased by the Nicholson Transit Company in 1925, and both vessels had been extensively modified and converted into automobile carriers.[1] Two new lower decks had been constructed within their cargo holds, below the main or spar deck. A midships elevator permitted new automobiles to be quickly lowered and parked, bumper to bumper, wheel to wheel. Dock workers would also fill the main deck with more cars. A typical cargo numbered approximately 250 vehicles.

At Detroit the *City of Bangor,* just out of the shipyard, where she had been given a new propeller shaft, had taken aboard 248 of Mr. Chryslers's newest cars, the "late" 1926's,

---

1 The *Penobscot* came to grief twenty-five years later when, in October of 1951, after delivering grain to Buffalo and outbound for a cargo of automobiles at Detroit, she collided with the gasoline tank barge *Morania* in Buffalo harbor. Eleven men perished, including the *Penobscot*'s skipper, Louis Guyette.

if you please. For in those days auto makers made major model changes in the spring, modest revisions in the fall.

Chrysler, the inventive, controversial, and enlightened engineer, had founded his company only two years earlier, in 1924. But already, with nearly fifty automobile manufacturers still in production, he was approaching fifth place in sales. Chryslers, auto buffs enthusiastically maintained, were always easy to start, a blessing not always consistent in many other makes. And the sleek new models aboard the *City of Bangor* incorporated still another Chrysler innovation, adjustable front seats.

The inherent problems of the *City of Bangor* were two. First, she, like many lake steamers of her era, was sadly underpowered for her length, which was 445 feet. Thrifty owners and canny naval architects, ever conscious of fuel consumption, were inclined to settle for steam plants that would provide a modest pace with a minimum of fuel consumed. This worked out efficiently under average weather conditions, but in really severe gales these underpowered vessels were inclined to blow around into the troughs of the seas without having enough power to regain their courses, imperiling both vessel and crew. And it goes without saying that owners and naval architects were rarely aboard under such conditions.

The second problem besetting the *City of Bangor* was that in the automobile trade, even when fully loaded the total burden was not enough to put the ship down anywhere near the steadying load line she was familiar with in the ore and coal traffic. She thus presented a high, vulnerable profile, making her easy prey to strong winds. This, compounded by her exceedingly modest 1235 indicated horsepower, presented an ominous potential under adverse conditions.

Having chosen to continue on past Whitefish Point, Captain Mackin, considering his vessel's restricted turning capabilities in high winds and seas, was really beyond the point of return. The next opportunity for shelter was at Bete Grise Bay, in the lee of Keweenaw Point, 147 miles of open water beyond Whitefish, the entire fetch exposed to winds building up for hundreds of miles over the Canadian prairie provinces. And blow they did, dusting the crown of the Sleeping Giant as they passed over Thunder Cape to pick up moisture from Lake Superior and become a howling blizzard.

But Keweenaw Point, offering quiet waters and good holding ground in her lee, can also clasp and hold in fatal embrace vessels that misjudge her hostile, rock-skirted coast. And in the dying days of November of 1926, before the era of ship-to-shore radio telephone and unbeknownst to Captain Mackin, Keweenaw and the south shore of Lake Superior had already exhibited the worst side of an often deplorable disposition. On the 26th the *Fordonian* went on a reef near the Huron Islands. Two days later the steamer *H. H. Hettler* drove ashore on Grand Island, near Munising, striking with such force that she was almost immediately abandoned to the underwriters. Earlier the sand-laden *Cottonwood* stranded on Keweenaw and, after an abortive salvage attempt, was likewise abandoned. Next, even as the *City of Bangor* fought her way toward Duluth, came the *Thomas Maytham*.

Ah, the *Thomas Maytham*, seemingly twice doomed.

Early in the month she had gone ashore on Knife Island, nineteen miles northeast of Duluth, and had apparently been badly damaged. But tugs had pulled her off, pumped her out, and escorted her to Superior, Wisconsin, for shipyard repairs. Once patched up she loaded grain for Toledo and departed. Her skipper, like Captain Mackin of the *City of Bangor*, was apparently convinced that the worst of a month of gales was over. But once beyond the Apostle Islands, with weather conditions worsening rapidly, the *Thomas Maytham*, also with limited horsepower, had little choice but to continue. With wind and sea from a following quarter harassing his vessel and driving her off course, her skipper could do naught but plug ahead, hoping to round the hook of Keweenaw and there to shelter in its lee.

Her crew sighing thankfully, the *Thomas Maytham* rounded Keweenaw Point and found relief from the force of the seas. But once in Bete Grise, blinded by the driving snow, her master miscalculated his position and put his vessel hard on a reef off Point Isabelle. She was still there, her crew safe but clamoring for rescue, when the *City of Bangor*, upbound, came abreast of Keweenaw Point, well offshore.

Captain Mackin, with visibility zero due to snow being driven before the renewed gale, kept his vessel steady on her course for Duluth and did a commendable job of it. He really had no choice, for the lights and beacons that could have directed him to shelter at Bete Grise Bay were invisible, lost in a swirling blanket of white. He had only his compass and known course to Duluth to guide him. He noted with some apprehension that the temperature was dropping rather sharply.

Eventually, and it was almost preordained as the gale continued to heighten, the steamer blew around too far and fell off into the troughs of the seas, seas that now clambered boisterously aboard with great regularity. A few moments later, as the helmsman fought to bring the steamer around on her course, the steam steering engine failed.

Rolling precipitously now, the *City of Bangor* began to divest herself of her deck cargo. Between intermittent flurries of snow, Captain Mackin watched sadly as some of Mr. Chrysler's splendid new automobiles went plummeting into the deep. Others, their wheels entangled in the cable-type railings, hung precariously, bashed about as the mounting seas assaulted them. Finally they, too, were plucked away and went to the bottom of Lake Superior. Altogether, Captain Mackin and his men counted eighteen of the automobiles lost to the insatiable, prowling grey-beards. Then, with the drop in temperature, both the vessel and her remaining deck cargo began to acquire a thin coating of ice.

Helpless, the *City of Bangor* was being driven relent-lessly toward Keweenaw, although the driving snow merci-fully hid its forbidding shoreline from the crew. As a mat-ter of fact, not a single man, including Captain Mackin or mates Smith and Luxton, knew exactly where they were. The snow and wind-driven spume had blotted out bearings for hours. Nor, considering the head seas they had encoun-tered constantly, could they judge the distance they had traveled.

"As luck would have it," recalls watchman Frank J.

Gerkowski,[2] "she picked the only shelving beach on the Point to go aground. A little one way or the other and we would have been under bluffs and would surely have lost our lives. We 'went on,' pounding and grinding, about dark and about seventy-five yards from shore. The seas were climbing right over us and making a regular maelstrom of the water and big rocks on our inshore side. We just had to stay put and pray that the ship didn't break up."

A large boulder had penetrated the bottom, aft, eventually flooding the boilers and engine room, thus depriving the vessel of heat. The seas continued to thunder against the port side, spewing tons of spume and spray down on the remaining deck cargo of automobiles. With the temperature now hovering near zero, ice began to build up rapidly.

"The aft and forward end crews were separated by the seas that kept climbing over us," Gerkowski remembers. "It was awfully cold for all of us up forward, including Captain Mackin, the mates, wheelsmen Harvey Nicholson [3] and Hugh Luxton,[4] along with George Lloyd, the other watchman, and myself. We spent the night huddled in the windlass room around a little fire we built from paneling we chopped from one of the rooms. The boys in the after end, snug and warm in the galley with heat from the coal range and plenty of food, had things much easier."

2 Frank J. Gerkowski, one of the *City of Bangor*'s watchmen, got his master's papers in 1939. Altogether, his sailing career in the Interlake, Reiss and Boland & Cornelius fleets spanned forty-two years.

3 Wheelsman Harvey Nicholson was the son of Frank Nicholson and nephew of William Nicholson, principal stockholder of the Nicholson Transit Company. Harvey continued his steamboat career and eventually became a shipmaster in his own right.

4 Wheelsman Hugh Luxton was a brother of second mate George Luxton.

Next morning the *City of Bangor* presented an awesome sight, more like an immense iceberg than a steamboat. Practically entombed in their quarters, the crewmen labored for several hours to chop open the doors. Everywhere there was ice, hundreds of tons of it, layered thick from smokestack to steering pole. The deckload of automobiles was a shapeless white mass. Worst of all, from the standpoint of help from an offshore vessel, prospects were dim. From out on the lake the white-sheathed *City of Bangor* blended perfectly into the snow-covered background of Keweenaw Point.

Captain Mackin had already determined that if they were to be saved it must be through their own efforts. He put his men to work chopping out the starboard lifeboat, freeing it and its releasing gear from a three-foot layer of ice. It was mid-afternoon when the task was done.

Captain Mackin's plan worked to perfection. A line secured to the lifeboat was laid out by those on deck. Another line was tied to the stricken steamer and coiled in the lifeboat. Then the lifeboat, with several crewmen aboard, was maneuvered to shore, where the end of the second line was fastened to a tree, well above the breaking seas. Then, by means of two more lines, one on the bow, the other on the stern, it was simply a chilly shuttle service back and forth until all twenty-nine men were ashore.

However, being ashore on the tip of Keweenaw Point was scarcely a comforting situation for men ill-equipped for temperatures below zero with a strong wind blowing. Before them lay a long, rough hike to the nearest settlement, the small village of Copper Harbor, where the few winter residents could be counted upon to provide food and shelter.

Only a handful of the crewmen had heavy clothing, but some cut blankets into strips, which they wrapped around their feet and legs. Off they went on a journey that, in good weather, would have brought them to Copper Harbor just in time for dinner. Instead of following the rugged shoreline, they chose to take a seemingly shorter route overland, through heavily timbered land and in snow that in places was waist deep.

But familiar landmarks seen from out on the lake took on foreign perspectives ashore. After trudging for miles in the cold and wind and with night closing in, they found themselves lost in a pine thicket. There was nothing to do but dig out fallen timbers and build a big fire to huddle around until dawn.

Completely discouraged and physically incapable of what seemed to be an endless march to Copper Harbor, they retraced their trail to the stranded steamer. Some, suffering from frostbite and fatigue, required help from shipmates better prepared for the icy December climate of the Keweenaw Peninsula. Arriving back at the site of the wreck late in the afternoon, they built another fire in an exposed area where its gleam and flare might arouse curiosity and eventual rescue. But it was a most disheartening situation.

Then occurred one of the more bizarre coincidences in Great Lakes history. Just when spirits were at their lowest ebb at the thought of another night of hunger and cold, around Keweenaw Point, homebound, chugged the thirty-six-foot double-ended Coast Guard motor lifeboat from

Eagle Harbor. With Captain Anthony F. "Tony" Glaza in command, the craft was returning from the east side of Keweenaw where it had picked up the crew of the stranded *Thomas Maytham*. It would be difficult to assess the feeling of Captain Glaza when, upon rounding the Point, he found still another wrecked steamer, her distressed crew obviously in need of immediate help.

The Coast Guard boat was already encrusted with ice and jammed to the grab rails with the *Thomas Maytham*'s people. There was no room for any of the *City of Bangor*'s men. Captain Glaza guided his craft to within hailing distance, and advised Captain Mackin that he would drop the *Maytham*'s crew at Copper Harbor and then return. Meanwhile, with the winter dusk already upon them, he asked that a large fire be kept burning to serve as a beacon, since it would necessarily be several hours before he could return.

Rescue came late that night, but not before several of Captain Mackin's crewmen suffered frozen hands and feet.

"Some of them, caught in the spray from the surf, had their clothes freeze to their bodies," recalls Frank Gerkowski.

Captain Glaza, as he promised, took the exhausted and hungry crew to Copper Harbor and almost at once departed for Eagle Harbor with the *Thomas Maytham*'s crew, leaving two of his men to administer first aid and arrange for food and shelter until he could return.

Food, warmth, and shelter were all forthcoming at the nearby Bergh farm, where Billy and Ida Bergh and their children welcomed twenty-nine strangers, most of whom immediately fell into a deep sleep on the floors, unmindful of growing puddles from ice melting from frozen clothing.

It was several days before the Coast Guard boat was able to return from Eagle Harbor. Meanwhile, the famished men devoured a substantial share of the Bergh's winter supplies, freely given and gratefully received.

But before Captain Glaza could get the *City of Bangor*'s men aboard his boat, a new gale arose, and before it subsided the double-ender was frozen in for the winter. The stranded mariners were eventually transported to Calumet by horse- and tractor-drawn sleighs and bobsleds. From there, on the South Shore Railway to connecting lines, they tardily found their way home in plenty of time for Christmas shopping.

Mid-December found underwriter's salvage crews at work on the wreck. Individual automobiles were chopped free from the deck and lowered by ramp to the now solid ice. Holes cut in the side of the steamer, with other ramps built to reach them, gave access to the two lower decks of automobiles. Then, over a road plowed out on the ice by teams of horses, the cars were driven one by one under their own power to a temporary rendezvous in Charley Maki's barnyard. Unfortunately, they were still twenty-nine miles from the railroad in Calumet, and the road between Copper Harbor and Calumet, never maintained in winter, boasted snow drifts ten feet high.

The *City of Bangor*, her salvage a doubtful possibility,[5]

---

[5] The *City of Bangor* spent the rest of her days silent and rusting just where she went ashore. There was much talk of salvage, but the problems were too great for a profitable operation. She lay there until World War II when her scrap value justified cutting her up.

was left to the cold and lonely darkness of winter on the rocky shore of the Keweenaw, there to muse at leisure with the bones of those who preceded her and to welcome new arrivals.[6]

In February, the Houghton County Road Commission crews under Thomas Coon and his assistant, William Kaiser, aided by Keweenaw County crews, began the assault on the road between Calumet and Copper Harbor.

"It took us three weeks, working practically around the clock," Kaiser recalls. "We set up camps along the road so the boys could get some rest off and on. Around Lake Medora and Brockway Mountain the snow was much higher than the equipment, even the big 'V' plows. Mixed into it were fallen trees and boulders. From Copper Harbor we had to clear a new, temporary road to where the cars were waiting. It was some kind of a 'first' for this part of the country."

Then, in an unprecedented but sporadic parade, the automobiles, chugging along between tremendous snowbanks, moved triumphantly to Calumet. Underwriters offered cash money for drivers—and found them, albeit many were under age, untested and absent from school.

Predictably, too, one or two cars managed to become misplaced. Some say they were legally purchased from the underwriters at bargain prices. Others, recalling oft-repeated yarns, seem to remember that they just became "lost" in the confusion.

But in any event, the underwriters and the Chrysler

6 The very next November, under strangely similar circumstances, the Canadian steamer *Altadoc* also went "hard on" Keweenaw. The crew was unaware of the location until a lull in the blizzard revealed the hulk of the *City of Bangor*, only a couple of hundred yards away.

people, considering that the entire salvage job had been a notable one under distressing circumstances, were not making a big issue out of a couple of strays. To this day, one of the strays is still around Calumet and in good working order, including the adjustable front seat.

Walter P. Chrysler always did make easy starting cars, and the late 1926's were no exception.

9

·
·
·
·

⚓

Was It One Whistle Signal
or Two?

In the usually barren and colorless rooms where duly
constituted authority in the form of steamboat inspectors
once gathered to pass judgment on the emergency decisions
of mariners, the state of existing weather conditions at the
time of a collision was often of paramount importance.[1]
And it was no less significant later in the more ornate federal courtrooms, when, the inspectors' findings being considered, damage or loss claims were either dismissed,
awarded to the plaintiff, or adjudicated on an equal-fault
basis.

In any event the state of the weather is more difficult to
assess in a courtroom than at sea, particularly when one or

[1] Until 1942, investigations of maritime mishaps were conducted by federal steamboat inspectors. The investigative authority was then assumed
by the United States Coast Guard, twenty-seven years after it succeeded
the old United States Lifesavings Service as the responsible agency for marine safety, rescue, and enforcement of operational procedures.

both shipmasters involved declare that it was "hazy." The term, often the subject of diametrically opposing testimony, is almost impossible to delineate, because *haze* means one thing to one person, something else—possibly fog—to another. Nevertheless, it is a frequent entry on ship's logs, even when only a light mist prevails. This is for the very practical reason that such a state of weather, there in black and white on the log, could possibly be a mitigating factor should some misadventure transpire while such conditions persist.

Unfortunately for those lost in marine accidents, the question of weather, be it fog, haze, darkness, storm, or a delightful day or night becomes a moot one. The weather no longer matters to them, nor do the official verdicts eventually rendered—not even when a shipmaster has been judged at fault.

Such a questionable state of weather existed, so one skipper said, when, at 9:10 P.M. on the evening of August 20, 1920, the steamers *Superior City* and *Willis L. King* collided in Whitefish Bay, on Lake Superior. The *Superior City* was downbound, heavy with 7600 tons of iron ore loaded at Two Harbors. The *Willis L. King*, light and with only water ballast, was upbound after unloading ore at Ashtabula, Ohio.

The weather existing at the moment quickly became academic for the *Superior City*'s second engineer, J. Espy Eagles; his wife, Jessie B. Eagles; and twenty-seven other members of the crew. Rammed on her port side, aft of midships, the *Superior City* sank rapidly, her passing hastened by a tremendous explosion when the terrible inrushing wall of cold water burst her aft bulkheads and hit the boilers. The vessel's stern was literally blown off while the crew members struggled to lower her lifeboats. Among those killed were three young Cleveland friends and neighbors, George Parker, Joseph Comyns, and Edwin Richardson. Parker had been saving most of his earnings for college tuition fees.

The survivors numbered only four, Captain E. L. Sawyer, second mate G. G. Lehne, watchman Peter Jacobsen, and boatswain Walter Richter. The first three were forward and jumped for their lives when the *Superior City* was nearly halved in the collision and were subsequently picked up by lifeboats from the *King*. Boatswain Walter Richter, asleep in his bunk at the time, dashed aft when the alarm bells rang, clad only in his long underwear. He, like others, was trying to help launch the boats when the explosion blew him overboard, at the same time relieving him of his underwear. He was naked as a jay bird when picked up by the steamer *J. J. Turner* twenty minutes later.

The collision quickly shaped up as a most curious affair when both masters, Captain Sawyer of the *Superior City* and Captain Herman J. Nelson of the *Willis L. King*, offered immediate but conflicting stories relative to the weather and whistle signals exchanged prior to the collision. At the Soo, where the *King* returned with considerable bow damage and the three *Superior City* survivors, Captain Nelson, despite the fact that his vessel had steamed directly into the port side of the *Superior City*, blustered, "Hell, I didn't hit her, she hit me!"

Whatever the circumstances, however, there were unprejudiced witnesses aboard two other vessels. The *J. J.*

Turner had been steaming downbound about twenty minutes behind the *Superior City*, and her officers observed the collision and sinking. So did the officers and crew of the *Midvale*, which had locked through the Soo behind the upbound *King* and was steaming somewhat aft and to the *King's* starboard side. Not only did they witness the collision, but they had heard the passing whistles exchanged.

Captain Sawyer told his owners, the Pittsburgh Steamship Company, that the weather was clear at the time of the accident, although there had been light fog or haze earlier in the evening. Captain Nelson held that the night had been foggy and hazy. The vessels had sighted each other some ten minutes before the collision, haze or no haze, and had exchanged passing signals with their steam whistles. Captain Sawyer maintained that he had blown one blast, the conventional port-to-port passing signal, to which the *King*, he said, responded with its own one-blast acknowledgement. Additional one-blast signals were repeated and answered, Captain Sawyer insisted, as the two vessels steamed ahead on what seemed as they neared each other, to be a collision course.

To the contrary, Captain Nelson and his officers and crew asserted, the signal from the *Superior City* had been two blasts, for a "two whistle" or starboard-to-starboard passing. Continued two-blast signals came from the *Superior City*, the captain insisted, until she "started to show me her red light" as she swung across the *King's* bow. And by this time, he stated, he had swung the bow of his vessel hard aport and rung the telegraph to "stop" and then "full astern." But of course it was too late, for the *King* plowed into the *Superior City*, cutting her nearly in two.

The estimated speed of the two vessels at the moment of impact was twelve miles per hour for the *King*, ten and one-half miles per hour for the *Superior City*.

After their initial statements given to federal steamboat inspectors Messrs. Charles M. Gooding and John Hansen at the Soo, both masters, aware that long and expensive litigation would likely result from their meeting in White-fish Bay, became very reticent, communicating only in depositions to the respective proctors-in-admiralty representing their respective owners, the Pittsburgh Steamship Company for the *Superior City* and the Interstate Steamship Company, owners of the *Willis L. King*.[2]

The search for possible survivors had begun almost immediately, the Lake Carriers' Association chartering the tug *L. C. Sabin* to patrol the area, while small craft hired by the Pittsburgh Steamship Company joined Coast Guard vessels to extend the search. But though a small armada combed Whitefish Bay for several days, the total yield was only a couple of shattered boards, probably the result of the explosion of the *Superior City*'s boilers.

Arriving at the Soo from Cleveland, Captain W. S. Smith, retired marine superintendent of the Pittsburgh Steamship Company, began an organized search, using as his base the Coast Guard vessel *Advance*. He also chartered

2 A strange fate befell twenty-month-old James Edward Eagles, orphaned when second engineer J. Espy Eagles and his wife, Jessie, were lost. (Mrs. Eagles was simply making a "courtesy" trip with her husband.) A judge, considering the welfare of young James Edward, ruled that he should spend six days a week with one pair of grandparents, the seventh day with the other grandparents.

Today, after long years of service, James Edward Eagles is a train dispatcher for the Norfolk & Western Railway Company. Approaching retirement, he is still puzzled and somewhat resentful of the judge's order. "It didn't make sense then," he says, "and it still doesn't."

a tug and indicated that he was prepared to spend at least two weeks searching every cove and inlet on the south shore of the Whitefish Bay area and also along the Canadian shoreline for wreckage of the vessel and the bodies of the twenty-nine victims. He asked for the cooperation of fishermen, advising them that the company would pay twenty-five dollars for the recovery of each body of the *Superior City*'s crew.

The official searchers returned from their quest empty-handed, but the unofficial searchers did not. A few days after the disaster, Robert F. Benjamin, chief engineer of another Pittsburgh Steamship Company vessel and brother of Jessie Eagles, got off his boat at the Soo to conduct his own search for his sister's body. He was joined by a brother, C. E. "Ed" Benjamin, Jr. They chartered the small motor vessel *Voyager* and began what was to become a ten-day expedition. Near Tequamenon Island, in Whitefish Bay, they discovered one hatch cover and a shattered lifeboat from the lost vessel. Working along the rugged shoreline, they had little trouble finding mute evidence of the violence of the explosion and the precipitous foundering of the ore-laden steamer. Although they located no bodies, they found a total of ninety-six hatch covers, a life raft, an icebox, life preservers, clothing, photographs, and the pilot house of the ill-fated *Superior City*, with Captain Sawyer's license still in its frame. They also made a point of interviewing all the area lighthouse keepers, confirming the fact that very early in the night of the collision there had indeed been haze and some fog on Whitefish Bay, but it had cleared and, for some time prior to the collision, the night had become crystal clear with unlimited visibility.

Back in Conneaut, Ohio, one young fellow, while mourning for his lost shipmates, could not but feel that Providence had given him special dispensation. Dick Leet was just another Conneaut boy who thought he wanted to make the Great Lakes his career. Second engineer Eagles had arranged to get him on the *Superior City* as an oiler. But while Leet did his work efficiently and willingly, engineer Eagles, aware that there was a certain young lady back in Conneaut, noted signs of homesickness and predicted in a letter to his mother that the young oiler would soon become disenchanted with shipboard life. "He's here on the boat," he wrote, "but his heart is back in Conneaut." Dick Leet did quit the vessel, on the trip before its final one.

After inspection and survey at the Soo, the *Willis L. King* was permitted to resume her voyage and steamed into Duluth-Superior harbor with her stem twisted, broken, and set back ten feet, seventeen shell plates and frames destroyed, interior forward decks buckled, and numerous angles and stringers that required replacement. She made immediately for the Superior Shipbuilding Company's drydock for repairs, with Captain Nelson ordering that no member of the crew was to leave the ship or discuss the accident with anyone but officials or representatives of the vessel's owners or agents. The shipbuilding company was asked to keep visitors away from the scene.

The mood of the shipping fraternity, not necessarily that of vessel owners but of working seamen, was expounded editorially by newspapers in all Great Lakes port cities, generally in the tenor expressed by Marquette's *Daily Mining Journal.* Said the paper:

It is a catastrophe that surely demands the close investigation it will now receive. The circumstances surrounding it are such as to compel the conclusion that in either craft, or both, there was inexplicable failure to comply with the rules the government has set up to make the lakes safe for mariners.

In view of massive evidence to the contrary, from the knowledgeable observers afloat, on shore, and in official capacities such as lightkeepers, Captain Nelson had quickly backed off from his original position that fog had been a factor. There was, as a further contradiction, his own statement, made soon after the accident, that both vessels had exchanged their original whistle signals when about four or five miles distant from each other. How could this have been had the night not been clear?

The wheels of justice grind exceedingly slow in admiralty affairs, and the *Superior City–Willis L. King* settlement was no exception. Owners of both vessels were privy to the services of the most prestigious and competent legal talent available and lost no time in availing themselves of such learned counsel. Numerous lawyers—or proctors, as they prefer to be termed in admiralty cases—responded with their accustomed vigor.

The federal steamboat inspectors, having conducted their own investigation but without the powers to rule on liability or subsequent litigation of damages, permitted witnesses such as the surviving *Superior City* crew members and the officers and crew of the *Willis L. King* to go about their business until such time as their testimony might be required in the courts.

Attorneys seeking additional statements and depositions had little trouble locating and interviewing the skippers involved—or the masters and officers of the *Midvale* or *J. J. Turner* when they docked at their usual ports of call.

It was a different matter in seeking audience with Peter Jacobsen, the *Superior City*'s watchman. Boatswain Walter Richter was promptly located, but Peter Jacobsen was a footloose fellow, true to the traditions of itinerant sailors, or "trippers," as their contemporaries were wont to call them.

Mr. Jacobsen was reported seen in various places and employed on a variety of vessels, but he always managed to be off on another wayward tack when attorneys thought they had him pinned down. One determined legal type assigned to get a deposition from Jacobsen began his task in early May of 1921, visiting the Cleveland offices of the Lake Carriers' Association to ascertain the watchman's present assignment. Luckless there, he next interviewed the personnel people of Hutchinson & Company, owners of the *Martin J. Mullen*, on which, it was rumored, Mr. Jacobsen was possibly currently employed. To that end he telephoned Buffalo to talk to the master of the *Mullen*, only to be told that the elusive Mr. Jacobsen was not presently bedding down in the *Mullen*'s fo'c'sle. By the middle of the month the attorney was back at the Lake Carriers' Association in the vain hope that their latest hiring records would reveal the watchman's assignment of the moment. This failing, he then personally interviewed the master of the *Mullen*, who, he thought, might have had some recent word on Jacobsen. In June the desperate attorney was in correspondence with legal representatives all around the lakes, seeking help in locating the reluctant Jacobsen, whose testimony might prove important in the upcoming

litigation. Still no luck. In the waning days of June he
was driven to a journey of desperation, rumor having it
that Jacobsen had "paid off" the *Mullen* in Buffalo and
was currently taking his ease in the favorite haunts of
sailors in that port. But if that was indeed the case, the
furtive watchman was exceedingly hard to find. The attorney spent four fruitless days at his task, itemizing time
spent in visiting the Seamen's Union and the Lake Carriers'
assembly room, making endless inquiries along the waterfront, and tramping from one sailor's boardinghouse to
another. Still Peter Jacobsen was nowhere to be found.

The task of interviewing witnesses, assembling the material, and compiling their respective legal briefs took the
proctors for both owners many months. The ultimate ob-
jective, of course, was to convince the judicial forces that
the respective skipper of the vessel whose owners they
represented was a sterling seaman, entirely guiltless of any
error of judgment in the course of events that resulted
in the sinking of the *Superior City*.

Because the *Willis L. King* had gone to Superior, Wisconsin, for her repairs, and since Superior was in the Western District of the United States District Court, proctors
for the *King* filed for limitation of liability proceedings in
Madison, Wisconsin, far from the freshwater lake where
the collision occurred. This shrewd strategic move was
made, so one of the proctors commented in correspondence
with the underwriters, "so as to get away from local Great
Lakes influence, the notoriety and comment by Great
Lakes newspapers. . . ."

In due time then, in the United States District Court,
the Western District of Wisconsin, and before Judge C.

Z. Luce, the Interstate Steamship Company, owners of the *King*, duly petitioned for limitation of liability.

Proctors for the petitioners, the firm of Holding, Masten, Duncan & Leckie, were distinguished in the field of admiralty law, as was the firm of Kelley & Cottrell, proctors for the claimants.

Captain Sawyer and his mate had earlier testified before the federal steamboat inspectors that the *Superior City* initiated the whistle signals, blowing one blast that was promptly acknowledged by the *King* with her own single blast. The *Superior City* then altered her course slightly to starboard. A short time later it was noticed by Captain Sawyer that the *King* was not responding in accordance with the passing agreement, whereupon, while still at a safe distance for passing, he blew another single blast, which was answered in kind by the *King*. Later on, it was said, as the *Superior City* altered still further to starboard, it appeared to those on board that the *King* was swinging to her own port and was following the *Superior City* around. Captain Sawyer then initiated another one-blast signal, together with the alarm signal, and swung his vessel's helm hard aport. His third one-blast signal was also answered by the *King*, which belatedly began swinging to her own starboard. But it was too late, the *King* crashing into the *Superior City* at 9:10 P.M. that fateful night.

The allegations of the petition for limitation of liability were supported by the testimony to the inspectors of Captain Nelson and several crew members of the *King*, which differed substantially from that of Captain Sawyer and second mate Lehne. While agreeing that the *Superior City* had initiated the series of whistles, the latter maintained that she blew *two* blasts. The *King*, they testified, returned the two-blast signal. A short time later, they affirmed, the *Superior City* blew another two-blast signal, acknowledged by a similar signal from the *King*, which maintained its course until the *Superior City* suddenly began to swing across toward the *King*. The *King* sounded the alarm signal, followed with a two-blast signal, and her engine was ordered stopped. The *Superior City*, they alleged, continued swinging across the *King*'s bow, whereupon the helm was thrown hard aport and a one-blast signal was blown. The *King*'s engine, by this time, was now working full astern.

All now agreed that though the early evening hours had been misty, hazy, and sometimes foggy, the night was perfectly clear at the time of the collision and the lights of all the vessels in the area, the *Superior City, Willis L. King, Midvale,* and *J. J. Turner* could be seen clearly. Significantly, both Captain Anderson and the mate of the *Midvale* gave testimony to the effect that the passing signal originating from the *Superior City* was *two* blasts, answered in kind by the *King*.

In the decision he rendered after much study and perusal of the evidence and testimony recorded by the federal steamboat inspectors, Judge Luce agreed that there was undoubtedly confusion over the passing signals and that both masters were guilty of not satisfying themselves as to the intent of the other, as required by the "Rules of the Road" regulations, and that under the circumstances they should have been more prudent. He cited the paragraph that covered just such contingencies and indicated that close attention to Pilot Rule Number 11 for the Great

Lakes would have prevented the collision. The rule reads as follows:

> If, when steamers are approaching each other, the pilot of either vessel fails to understand the course or intention of the other, whether from signals being given or answered erroneously, or from other causes, the pilot so in doubt shall immediately signify the same by giving the DANGER SIGNAL or four or more short and rapid blasts of the whistle; and if both vessels shall have approached within half a mile of each other, both shall be immediately slowed to a speed barely sufficient for steerageway, and, if necessary, stopped and reversed, until the proper signals are given, answered, and understood, or until the vessels shall have passed each other.

Judge Luce also noted the testimony that at no time during the emergency had Captain Sawyer cut down the speed of the *Superior City*. The telegraph had remained at "full ahead" and was still in that position when the vessel sank. Captain Sawyer maintained that to have stopped and reversed his engine at the time when the hard aport order was given and the alarm sounded would not have avoided the collision. Other witnesses corroborated his position. Judge Luce was inclined to agree but wrote,

> I am persuaded that he was in doubt about the course of the *King* prior to blowing the alarm and ordering his helm hard aport and in ample time to have slowed his speed, given the alarm and stopped, so that the collision would have been avoided.

But on that tragic night of August 20, 1920, the wisdom of Pilot Rule Number 11 had not prevailed.

Further from Judge Luce:

I am convinced that each boat had the other on its starboard bow, that they were in relative positions propitious for a starboard to starboard passing, and there was no necessity for any change. However, the *King* gave its assent to the change, and if initiating such a change were a fault on the part of the *Superior City,* the *King* concurred in it and it became incumbent upon the latter to direct her course accordingly. This was not done, and in this the *King* was at fault.

"I therefore hold," Judge Luce concluded, "that both vessels were at fault and decree accordingly, providing for a division of damages."

But by now it was January of 1923 and to the twenty-nine people of the *Superior City* who still lay in Lake Superior's frigid depths it mattered not who blew steam whistles or how many times they were blown. As a point of fact, it made no difference the night of the collision.

Underwriters, again represented by distinguished proctors, haggled over the value of the *Superior City.* Her owner's representatives, in calculating her worth at twenty-two years of age, talked of from $450,000 to $475,000 but agreed, finally, to a figure of $300,000. Messrs. Holding, Masten, Duncan & Leekie, proctors representing the owners of the *King,* suggested a much lower valuation, $250,000. There could be little dispute on the insurance on the last cargo. Determining its value was a simple matter of multiplying the tonnage by the cost of ore per ton at the time—the total came to $42,922.95. Nor was there room for argument as to the extent of the *King*'s damage, the $26,520 in repair bills speaking for themselves.

But in the early 1920s—and the *Superior City*'s loss-of-life claims were not paid until late in 1923, the valuation placed on human lives was much more negotiable than that of sunken steamboats, lost cargoes, or damages to vessels. Administrators of the estates of the *Superior City's* victims had lawyers, too, but they had little muscle against the legal maneuverings of experienced admiralty proctors. The attorneys filed suits for specific amounts in every instance but were, of course, offered settlements at much lower figures. They had a choice of accepting the proffered settlements or being faced with the "burden of proof" requirements, which would inevitably have involved protracted and expensive litigation with no assurance of a more satisfactory figure.

Minnie E. Ferguson, wife of chief engineer George S. Ferguson, sued for $40,000 and settled for $25,000. Administrators of the estates of J. Espy Eagles, second engineer, and his wife, Jessie, sued for $30,000 for each of the deceased. They settled for $11,250 in the death of the engineer, $3,750 for the loss of Mrs. Eagles. The families of the three young Cleveland pals, porter George W. Parker, deckhand Joseph Comyns, and porter Edwin J. Richardson, all of whom earned $95 a month on the *Superior City*, each sued for $10,400 but agreed to accept $5000.

So it went, down the line for all twenty-nine victims. Perhaps the most grateful of all for not burdening his loved ones with the long proceedings was young Dick Leet, the homesick oiler from Conneaut who quit the *Superior City* the trip before she went down.

A strange epilogue became part of the *Superior City* legend, a poignant ritual of love and respect. It concerns Robert F. Benjamin, brother of Jessie B. Eagles, the man who left his post as chief engineer of another Pittsburgh

Steamship Company vessel to search for his sister and brother-in-law in Whitefish Bay. Although he sailed for many years after the tragic collision, whenever his steamer was in the vicinity of the *Superior City*'s watery grave, he would leave his engine room or quarters and stand on the vessel's fantail, peering out over the waters of Whitefish Bay where his loved ones had gone down with their ship. The silent vigil of Robert F. Benjamin is still recalled by James Edward Eagles, who was only twenty months old when his parents perished and nearly five years old when the *Superior City*'s final affairs were settled.

"It wasn't something he had to do," says Eagles. "It was something he wanted to do. Who knows what thoughts and memories flooded back in his mind. They were his own, and his shipmates respected his need for those quiet moments alone out there on the after deck."

10

·
·
·
·

⚓

A Captain's Farewell

Captain Louis Guyette and Torbjorn Sorensen, complete strangers, met quite by accident one night—met where the Buffalo River meets the outer harbor and where, under normal circumstance, the occasion would call for nothing more than a friendly wave of the hand or the wink of a flashlight.

But the fact remains that their encounter, at 9:20 P.M. on the evening of October 29, 1951, triggered off a waterfront inferno that doomed eleven seamen, periled many others, and also provided a classic instance of ships that *did not* pass in the night.

Still there were elements of Longfellow's immortal words that held true:

> Ships that pass in the night,
> and speak to each other in passing,
> Only a signal shown
> and a distant voice in the darkness;

In the meeting of Captains Guyette and Sorensen and their respective vessels, there were indeed distant voices in the darkness, many of them, but the question of signals, visual and audible, was one that inspired some controversy and reassessment of existing regulations.

Ironically, it was a whim of weather that provided the primary element of the drama, although at the time of the meeting the night was clear, visibility good, and a south-southwest wind of twenty-miles-per-hour prevailed. Actually it was a quirk of weather a day earlier that decreed that Captains Guyette and Sorensen would have their fateful rendezvous where and when they did.

Captain Sorensen, skipper of the diesel tug *Dauntless No. 12*, had departed Toledo towing the 230-foot tank barge *Morania No. 130*. His destination was Tonawanda, New York, along the Black Rock Canal where, at the Hambelton Terminal Corporation, the barge's 19,200 barrels of gasoline would be pumped out. It was entirely a routine operation.

But when loaded the *Morania* offered only three and one-half feet of freeboard, and in any kind of blustery weather she was indeed a "wet craft." Furthermore, with her broad, scow-like bow, she tended to be a bit sluggish under such conditions and difficult to handle. Consequently, when a storm developed and showed no signs of being merely a temporary caprice of nature, Captain Sorensen hauled around to starboard and took refuge in the fine, large natural harbor at Erie, Pennsylvania. It chanced to be a quiet Sabbath in the city, and both vessels and their crews settled down in the lee of Presque Isle Peninsula for a full twenty-four hours, "waiting for weather."

When better weather developed and forecasts for more of the same were received, the *Dauntless* took the *Morania* on a short line and departed Erie, lengthening the towline once out into the open waters of Lake Erie.

It was Monday, now, and the tug and barge were a day behind their projected schedule. In the movement of Great Lakes cargoes weather is frequently an erratic factor, and such delays are accepted as an inherent and unpredictable part of the shipping business. But in this case it meant that it was Monday night instead of Sunday night when the *Dauntless* slowly pulled her consort around the corner of Buffalo's "old" breakwater. Then, after hauling to starboard in sheltered waters and taking the way off the *Morania*, Captain Sorensen set about rearranging his tow.

In close quarters or confined waterways the *Dauntless* shifted from her normal practice of towing the *Morania* astern. Instead, she came around, fitted her nose into the "V"-shaped stern of the barge, and literally anchored herself in that position by tightening cables fastened to the outboard "wing" cleats or bollards on the *Morania*. This made for a compact and more maneuverable "pusher" tow.

Thus prepared, the *Dauntless*, preceded by the low, dark hull of the *Morania*, began her approach to the Buffalo River, slightly westward of the entrance. Captain Sorensen planned to take his integrated unit only a short distance up the river before hauling sharply to port and into the Erie Basin where, protected by another breakwater, he could begin transit of the Black Rock Canal to his destination.

As it chanced, the Buffalo River, just above the point

where Captain Sorensen would make his entrance, was
presently occupied by the slow-moving outbound steamer
Penobscot, Captain Louis Guyette in command.

The *Penobscot,* an automobile-grain carrier, had completed delivery of 200,000 bushels of grain to Pillsbury's
Mutual Elevator along the Buffalo Ship Canal and was
outbound for Detroit, where a cargo of automobiles
awaited delivery to Duluth.

The *Penobscot* had been snaked away from her elevator
moorings by a Great Lakes Towing Company tug and been
dragged sternwise to the nearby turning basin, at which
point the tug had quickly taken a bow line to line the vessel up with the outer harbor pier lights. Captain Guyette
had approved the operation, tooting on the whistle for the
tug to cast off the tow line once the steamer was in control
of her own destiny.

The unfolding tragedy was really one of built-in factors,
some beyond control of those soon to become intimately
involved in a disaster almost preordained by time and circumstances. And time, in this instance, reflected most importantly on the twenty-four hours the *Dauntless* and *Morania* had been weather-bound at Erie.

The *Dauntless,* pushing the dark hull of the *Morania,*
slowly rounded the bulkheading on the west side of the
entrance to the river channel, unaware of the nearby
Penobscot. Captain Sorensen, unaccountably, did not give
the required signal blast warning of a vessel approaching
an area of potential danger. Captain Guyette of the *Penobscot* did, although this precautionary signal in no way
altered the subsequent developments.

In all fairness, each master was a victim of circumstances.

Captain Sorensen, fully expecting a clear channel, maneuvered the *Dauntless* and *Morania* around the projecting bulkheads along the south bank of the Buffalo River at a cautious pace. But his vision was obstructed by the United States Coast Guard station and its ancillary structures, built at the very tip of the juncture of the river and outer harbor. This probably prevented him from observing the red port running light of the *Penobscot*. Furthermore, the steamer's high masthead lights would have been lost and obscured by the maze of lights in the background, those from the high buildings and business district of the city.

From the *Penobscot*, the Coast Guard station structures would have hidden the running lights of the *Dauntless*. But most of the unlighted bulk of the *Morania* was already in the channel and plodding slowly upstream, across the course of the *Penobscot*. Strangely, the absence of signal or port-and-starboard lights on the bow of the *Morania* did not constitute a violation of regulations. This amazing rule of inland waterways navigation, as baffling to small-craft operators on the western rivers as it sometimes is to Great Lakes mariners, resulted in the bulk of the *Morania* actually being in the navigable area of the Buffalo River before the required running lights on her *after* end became visible. Her low, dark profile, with only three and one-half feet of freeboard, was thus mostly indistinguishable from the vantage point of the *Penobscot*'s pilot house.

Captain Guyette had signaled for the tug to release the tow line and was lining up the steering pole between the pier lights when the impending tragedy began to take final form.

Seaman Albert Reid was in the windlass room of the

steamer, pulling in the towing hawser. Third mate Stanley Kielbasa was on the fo'c'sle deck at the bow, as lookout, at the same time supervising the job of hawser retrieval when he saw the shadowy form of the *Morania* angling across the channel.

"He's coming across," Kielbasa yelled to the pilot house.

At the same instant Captain Sorensen, at once aware of the situation, blew two whistles, indicating that he was intending to cross the *Penobscot*'s bow for a starboard-to-starboard passing, and simultaneously signaled his engine room for full speed ahead. But, of course, it was too late.

In the pilot house of the *Penobscot*, moments after Captain Guyette had blown the traditional and required danger signal at the approach of a dangerous channel intersection, the skipper instantly appraised the situation as hopeless, blew one more warning whistle and then followed with the emergency signal, a series of rapid blasts. At the same time, he swung the engine room telegraph to "full astern."

What was to happen was already destined by the momentum or "way" of the respective vessels, particularly of the *Penobscot*.

At about twenty minutes after nine o'clock that fateful Monday night, the stem of the outbound steamer struck the side of the gasoline-laden *Morania*, holing Number Five and Six tanks on the barge's starboard side. Instantly thousands of gallons of gasoline began gushing out, covering the water with an explosive and flammable coating and filling the air with explosive vapors.

Seaman Albert Reid, in the windlass room retrieving the tow line, watched the impending disaster through a porthole, saw the *Morania* alongside, and then felt the shock of the collision. He slammed shut the porthole, grabbed a life ring, and hastened aft. So did third mate Kielbasa, after a visit to the windlass room, where the odor of gasoline was almost overpowering. He was followed by second mate Edward Homeier, who was in his pajamas and had been about to climb into his bunk.

Then, as in the words of Longfellow, there were distant voices in the darkness, most of them shouting, "Gas, don't light any matches!"

Homeier, when he gained the after end and descended into the engine room, instructed the duty crew to keep the *Penobscot*'s engine in reverse.

The oft-shouted warning not to light matches was really an automatic reaction. As the *Penobscot* and *Morania* twisted and drew apart, the grating and grinding of torn plates provided the spark that ignited the gasoline vapors. An explosion blew burning gasoline over the *Penobscot*, *Morania*, and *Dauntless* and quickly turned the Buffalo River into an inferno. Quickly spreading over the surface of the water, the flaming gasoline instantly engulfed the barge, tug, and forward end of the *Penobscot*.

Captain Guyette's last act, before he and wheelsman Roy Richardson were incinerated, was to blow the abandon ship signal on his vessel's whistle—one long blast. Richardson, his shipmates were convinced, turned the wheel so that the vessel's stern would touch the south bank, where they could be saved.

But the forward momentum of the steamer temporarily kept her in the pool of flames, now shooting fifty feet into the air. Only after the engine, still reversed, backed her upstream, did the *Penobscot* draw away from the flames. Then her stern hit the Coast Guard wharf, damaging her rudder. At this moment, a rope was thrown from the fantail of the ship to the Coast Guard dock, and down it slid Albert Reid, Edward Meiers, Alfred Randa, and second mate Homeier. All the forward crew, with the exception of wheelsman Richardson and Captain Guyette, managed to retreat to the after end of the *Penobscot*. Among them was first mate Russell Woodward, who had gone below to inspect the damage and was literally blown out of the forepeak. Somewhere along the line of escape, he suffered an eye injury.

Some, including brothers James and Joseph Hassett, attempted to launch a lifeboat. But the boat suddenly stopped and tipped, tossing them into the river. A tug then pulled alongside, rescuing those spilled from the boat and others who clambered down from the *Penobscot*.

Meanwhile, almost total annihilation was the fate of the crew of the *Dauntless*, caught in the vortex of the explosion and geyser of burning gasoline. Gone were chief engineer Emil Emig; his assistant, Clifford Rank; cook Arthur Reilly; oiler Walter Brown; and deckhands Harold Holt and Alfred Aarseth.

Strangely, both Captain Sorensen of the *Dauntless* and Captain Lars Stromsland of the *Morania* found themselves in the water, swimming furiously away from the flames. Captain Stromsland found Captain Sorensen in a life preserver that also supported the tug's first mate, George Van Steenburg. All three then clung to the buoyant life preserver until a small tug spotted them. But moments before rescue, mate Van Steenburg slipped away and was gone.

Olav Gulliksen, the *Morania*'s first mate, was seen swimming in the flaming gasoline but soon disappeared.

Buffalo patrolmen Arnold Andres and Ralph Lickfield, cruising near the waterfront, witnessed the explosion and the rapid spread of the fire. The alarm they turned in brought downtown fire equipment to the scene.

But land-based apparatus was quite helpless, since the current had by now carried all three vessels away from piers and docks. Coast Guard vessels and the Buffalo fireboat *W.S. Grattan* arrived and began throwing streams of water and chemicals on the flaming hulls. The tugs *North Carolina, Ohio,* and *California* rushed from their Great Lakes Towing Company moorings to search for victims and assist wherever they could.

For WBEN-TV it was one of those rare examples of a scoop on a breaking news story. With a clear view of the disaster scene from its eighteenth-floor studios of the Hotel Statler, the station televised an on-the-spot spectacular that kept thousands of Buffalonians glued to their sets.

The flames on the *Penobscot* and *Dauntless* were extinguished rather promptly; the barge *Morania* burned for nearly twelve hours, but consuming only the gasoline in the ruptured tanks and leaving 90 per cent of her cargo still confined to her other tanks. She was, in the words of Buffalo port authorities, still a virtual "time bomb." They later arranged for the remaining cargo to be pumped out.

Buffalo hospitals, meanwhile, had been treating *Penobscot* crewmen for various injuries, shock, and minor burns.

All were vociferous in their praise for Captain Guyette and wheelsman Richards for sticking to their posts and backing the stricken steamer from the pool of flames.[1]

"We wouldn't have made it without them," said fireman Albert Hayden, who had been spilled from the malfunctioning lifeboat. "Now they're dead and we survived."

Surprisingly, a number of the *Penobscot*'s crew, because the fire had been confined to the forward end and was contained there, either stayed aboard their vessel or returned as soon as they were treated and released from the hospitals. They stood in silent, sorrowing clusters as firemen removed the bodies of Captain Guyette and wheelsman Richardson.

Bad news travels fast, necessarily in many cases, and while the *Penobscot* was still burning, her Buffalo agent phoned her owners, the Nicholson Transit Company in Detroit. Nicholson people immediately called their legal representatives, the prestigious firm of admiralty attorneys Foster, Meadow and Ballard, whose offices were, coincidentally, in the Penobscot Building.

---

[1] Sailors, most of them being of a superstitious bent, are forever conscious of strange or unusual coincidences. And in the passing of Captain Guyette they found what they perceived to be an omen of preordanied tragedy.

Captain Guyette had once been a skipper in the Minnesota Atlantic Transit Company fleet, best known in the marine faternity as the "Poker Fleet," due to management's penchant for naming their vessels after playing cards. For years their *Ace, King, Queen, Jack, Ten,* and *Nine* sailed the lakes in the package freight business. Now it was observed that past skippers of the line were prone to fatal accidents. Captain James Mac-Donald was in Duluth, walking back to the *Ace,* when he was struck by an automobile and killed instantly. Captain Archibald Maclean, as chief mate aboard a convoy during World War II, was lost when his ship was torpedoed. Captain John Heaney was fatally injured in an automobile accident in Detroit. And now, of course, there was brave Captain Louis Guyette.

The presence of a member of the firm on the disaster scene was, of course, practically mandatory. The task fell, late that night, to Charlie Meadows, who, under the circumstances, would much rather have stayed in Detroit. The Meadowses were momentarily expecting the arrival of a new family member. But duty called, and Charlie Meadows went pelting off to Buffalo to put the nautical legalities and other unpleasant affairs of the *Penobscot* in order. And while he was gone, little Janet Lynn Meadows came into the world.

The facts and factors leading to the fiery collision came out in due time—and in this instance it did not take long—before a marine board of investigation. The board concluded that while the Coast Guard station and its ancillary structures did indeed obstruct the view of the Buffalo River from the angle approached by the *Dauntless*, the tug's master was guilty of two specific violations involving navigation in congested and confined waterways. First, he did not, as required by regulations, have a lookout posted on the bow of the *Morania*, there to warn of converging traffic. Secondly, he had not blown the required warning blast on the tug's whistle as he prepared to turn into the river from the outer harbor.

On the other hand, Captain Guyette had blown a warning whistle 1500 feet before reaching the juncture of the river and outer harbor. Moreover, the *Penobscot* had third mate Stanley Kielbasa as lookout on the fo'c'sle deck.

It was, then, the board's considered opinion that the collision was primarily the fault of Captain Sorensen for proceeding to enter the Buffalo River from a blind spot without first ascertaining whether this was safe from the possi-

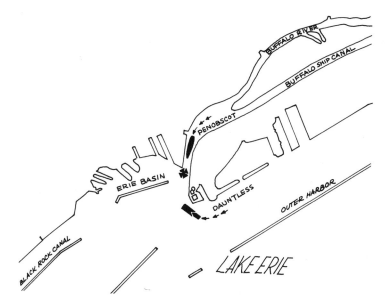

Map by Vincent Matteucci
Without warning whistles from the tug *Dauntless,* and the lack of a watchman on her deck, the collision with the *Penobscot* was almost inevitable.

bility of outbound traffic. His failure to post a lookout and blow a warning signal were contributory factors.

However, Captain Guyette and wheelsman Richardson were beyond the earthly sphere of hearings, depositions, testimony, and decisions. Nor could they hear the words of praise and gratitude from their shipmates on the old *Penobscot.* Walt Whitman, perhaps speaking for all stricken seamen, said it all:

> I with mournful tread,
> Walk the deck my Captain lies,
> Fallen cold and dead.

11

.
.
.
.

⚓

A Stranger on the Life Raft

Among the more appreciative users of Alexander
Graham Bell's marvelous invention are Great Lakes sailors.
Unlike their saltwater contemporaries, often oceans apart
from their homelands, freshwater seamen are able to call
home with some frequency. Thus, late on the dark and
gusty night of Saturday, November 25, 1966, when the ore-
laden *Daniel J. Morrell* eased quietly through the south
entrance of the Buffalo breakwater and crept slowly into
the long dock of the Bethlehem Steel Corporation's sprawl-
ing works at Lackawanna, numerous crewmen beat a path
to the public telephone at the far end of the dock.

Among the callers were wheelsman Charles H. Fosbender, watchman Dennis Hale, coalpasser Saverio Grippi,
and fireman Arthur Fargo. Others, such as wheelsman
Henry Rischmiller, fireman Chester Koniecska, deckhand
Arthur Stojek, steward Stanley Satlawa, and porter Charles
Sestakauskas, all residents of Buffalo or nearby communities, quickly dispersed for short visits at home. This happy

respite was possible because two vessels were already at the dock awaiting their turns under the four Hulett unloaders. Based on previous experience, the *Morrell's* crewmen calculated, optimistically perhaps, that their vessel would be in port for at least twenty-four hours. Creeping in behind the *Daniel J. Morrell*, her dark hull glistening in the flare of the coke ovens, came the *Edward Y. Townsend*, beaten to a berth by a scant hour.

Dennis Hale's call to his home in Ashtabula, Ohio, was to inform his wife that he would be home soon, the 114-mile trip made possible because the frequency of the *Morrell's* trips to Lackawanna justified leaving his Buick station wagon parked near the dock. A passenger would be deck watchman John Groh, who would be dropped off at the Harbor Creek, Pennsylvania, interchange on Route 90. They arranged to meet at the same place for the return trip to the steamer. It was Hale's third season as a sailor, all aboard the *Morrell*. He was actually unenthusiastic about shipboard life and the long intervals away from home. However, two previous jobs as a chef had evaporated, and with a wife and four children to provide for, he had decided that sailing was better, much better, than being unemployed. Winters he spent with repair gangs in nearby Conneaut, Ohio, working on vessels of the United States Steel Corporation fleet.

Fellow Ashtabulans whose duties kept them aboard or near the *Morrell* were fireman Arthur Fargo and coalpasser Saverio Grippi. But they, too, called home. Grippi spoke to his wife, Sarah, and Fargo to his wife, Nellie. Grippi had previously expressed displeasure because he so often found their party line busy. So he had ordered private service installed. Both men were unhappy, not only about not getting home, but about an unfortunate change of plans that affected the entire crew. Fargo had been a member of the *Morrell*'s crew for only nineteen days, having been hastily recruited after his predecessor had "gone astray" in pursuit of shore-side pleasures while the vessel was unloading iron ore in Ashtabula.

Captain Arthur I. Crawley phoned his home in Rocky River, Ohio, where he lived with his widowed sister, Mrs. Mary Reidy, and his brother John. "It's been a strenuous season," he told them, "and I'll welcome the opportunity to return home."

The fateful change of plans came in a message received by Captain Crawley when the *Morrell* was loading iron ore at Taconite Harbor, Minnesota. The message was from the vessel's Cleveland headquarters, advising him that at least one more trip would be required to meet tonnage commitments. The crew, assuming that they were on the last leg of their final seasonal trip, were, to say the least, disappointed. Two firemen registered their displeasure by quitting as soon as the *Morrell* docked at Lackawanna, as did deckhand Mark Petroff. All three were paid off by first mate Phil Kapets. Milo Becker, an oiler, also left the boat, but because of illness at home.

Technically, for tax purposes perhaps, the *Daniel J. Morrell* was officially recorded as being owned by the Cambria Steamship Company, but she was operated by the Great Lakes Steamship Division of the Bethlehem Steel Corporation. It mattered little to her crewmen what name was imprinted on their paychecks as long as they were negotiable.

The added trip changed many plans. Like others, wheelsman Fosbender was disgruntled. His call home to St. Clair, Michigan, was to inform his wife, Jan, that he would not be home as soon as he had anticipated. Wheelsman Stuart T. Campbell, of Marinette, Wisconsin, did likewise. It was particularly disappointing to Campbell, for he had intended to retire immediately after lay-up chores had been completed. Otherwise, those crewmen of the *Morrell* not required to maintain steam or keep deck watch, vanished to the haunts favored by sailors far from home with time on their hands—shopping for personal necessities, seeking out a late movie, or just whiling away the hours in a friendly tavern, of which Lackawanna and nearby Buffalo had an ample supply.

Meanwhile, Dennis Hale sped homeward to Ashtabula, blissfully unaware that fate would soon single him out as leading character in one of the grimmest dramas in Great Lakes history. Nor could he have known that a haunting, ghostly, white-haired stranger would play a major supporting role. At the moment, happily chatting with John Groh, knowledge of what was to come would have seemed too bizarre to be believable.

The plans of sailors have a much more consistent record of going awry than those of other men. When Hale and Groh wheeled briskly into the dock area at Lackawanna on their return Sunday night, they were approximately one hour late. The masthead lights of the *Daniel J. Morrell* were slowly swinging in an arc as the vessel steamed out the south entrance of the Buffalo breakwater. The *Edward Y. Townsend* had taken her place at the ore dock and the big Huletts were already chewing away at her cargo.

Momentarily stunned by the unfortunate turn of events, including the very real possibility of being denied their end-of-season bonuses, the pair conferred on possible solutions before uniting on a course of action. They drove to the Buffalo Coast Guard Station where, after explaining their dilemma, they were put in touch with the *Morrell* through the station's ship-to-shore radio telephone.

Captain Crawley was understanding. "We'll be taking on coal bunkers at the Mullen Dock in Windsor," he advised. "You can get back aboard there."

Without wasting a moment, the pair started back to Ashtabula, where Hale arranged for friends to drive them to Windsor. Exactly three hours after the tardy sailors left the Coast Guard station, at 3:10 A.M., the last of the *Edward Y. Townsend's* ore cargo was snatched from her holds, the "clean up" rigs hoisted out, and her lines cast off. Then, like the *Morrell*, she backed cautiously out the short canal, turned slowly, and lined up with the south breakwater opening. Steering midway between Waverly and Seneca shoals, the *Townsend* began her journey the length of Lake Erie. Like the *Daniel J. Morrell*, she had one more trip for the season.

There was a bit of slop running on the lake that night. Aboard the *Daniel J. Morrell*, after entering "Trip No. 34" in the log and checking the course, Captain Crawley found it expedient to get some sleep.

Captain Crawley, "Art" to hundreds of friends, was somewhat of an enigma. Like Dennis Hale he was rather an unenthusiastic sailor, a fact not consistent with the years of conscientious effort expended in rising from deckhand to master. Times were hard and jobs scarce in 1937, when he shipped out on the *Lebanon* the day after he graduated from Cleveland's St. Ignatius High School. Strangely, because of something he was never able precisely to delineate, he stayed on, slowly climbing the ladder of shipboard authority.

"There comes a day," he once confided to a friend, "when you realize that you have too much time invested, too much equity, so to speak, to make a change."

Captain Crawley began the season of 1966 with his first command, and, oddly, it was the old *Lebanon*, the very vessel on whose decks he began his career. But in August the retirement of another master and a resulting shuffle of commands in the Bethlehem fleet moved Captain William L. Hull from the *Morrell*, and Captain Crawley was named to replace him.

Entirely consistent with his own philosophy, although it was within his power to help them, Captain Crawley had steadfastly discouraged his eager nephews from becoming sailors, although they expressed a strong interest in Great Lakes careers. "It's a lonely life, boys," he counseled them, "and after wasting a few years, you'll find out that this isn't the life for you."

Four men short of her usual crew complement of thirty-three, although still adequately manned according to Coast Guard regulations, the sixty-year-old *Daniel J. Morrell* maintained her usual sedate pace the 235 miles from Buffalo light without incident. At nine o'clock on the morning of the twenty-seventh, Captain Crawley routinely reported via radio telephone to dispatcher Roy Dobson in the Cleveland office of the Bethlehem fleet that he was due at Detroit about 7:00 P.M. that night. But his plans to dock on schedule for bunker fuel at Windsor's Mullen Dock proved to be too optimistic. Choppy seas, snow flurries, and strong adverse winds prompted him to anchor in the lower Detroit River at dusk to await more favorable conditions, or at least until he had the benefit of daylight. This fact he duly reported to Mr. Dobson.

Shortly after ten o'clock that night, the *Edward Y. Townsend* passed her anchored sister ship. Captain Thomas J. Connelly and Captain Crawley, fast friends for years, communicated via radio telephone and discussed the weather conditions that might be expected on Lake Huron. They did not like the looks of the reports they had been receiving, and Captain Connelly advised his friend that he intended to anchor in the upper St. Clair River. The *Townsend* continued on, eventually dropping her anchor below Stag Island at four o'clock the next morning. It had been a long night for Captain Connelly.

Dennis Hale and John Groh arrived at the Mullen Dock early on the evening of Monday, the twenty-seventh, but found that their boat had obviously been delayed. They found shelter in one of the dock offices, from where they kept a sharp eye open for the familiar lights of the *Morrell*, now considerably overdue. Actually the vessel was anchored only ten minutes steaming time from the dock, but she might as well have been ten hours away. At five minutes to seven the next morning, Captain Crawley heaved anchor and proceeded to the dock, there to take on 221 tons of coal bunkers and his two tardy crewmen. The *Morrell* departed the fuel dock at exactly 7:30 A.M. Twenty-three minutes later the J. W. Westcott ship-reporting agency logged her as passing Detroit, a fact that Captain

Crawley also reported to dispatcher Dobson an hour later. At one o'clock that Tuesday afternoon, the *Daniel J. Morrell* passed the *Edward Y. Townsend*, which lay still snug at anchor below Stag Island. Captain Connelly had been listening to radio conversations between vessels on Lake Huron, trying to get some indication of on-the-scene weather in the southern reaches of the lake. What he heard was not reassuring.

Weather Bureau forecasts, which became effective at noon that day, called for gale warnings with northeasterly winds at thirty-four to forty knots, occasionally forty-one to forty-seven knots the following twelve hours. Snow, or rain and snow were predicted for the next twenty-four hours. Radio conversations monitored by Captain Connelly indicated that the predictions were accurate. Moreover, the same conditions were predicted for the succeeding twenty-four hours.

At the time he heaved anchor, shortly before three o'clock that afternoon, a conversation overheard by Captain Connelly indicated that the winds in southern Lake Huron were still relatively mild, six to twenty-eight miles per hour. He also initiated a call to the *Daniel J. Morrell,* which by this time was out on Lake Huron in the vicinity of the Lake Huron lightship. Weather was the topic of conversation.

Later, when the *Townsend* was abeam of Harbor Beach, following the recommended upbound track on the chart, the two skippers talked again. The *Daniel J. Morrell* was almost two hours ahead of the *Edward Y. Townsend,* and Captain Crawley reported that the wind was northerly, at about thirty-five miles per hour and increasing rapidly.

The seas were also northerly, estimated to eight feet and building with crests approximately 250 to 300 feet apart. Still later, at ten o'clock that night, they conferred again about the weather, which was deteriorating rapidly, with winds at fifty miles per hour and northerly seas now at twelve feet.

The *Edward Y. Townsend*, although previously riding fairly well, now started to pound and roll, inspiring Captain Connelly to restrict movement of personnel between the forward and after sections of his vessel. He feared that the wind and seas might cause his vessel to broach or be blown around into the troughs of the seas, which would then inevitably sweep the deck. In one of the earlier conversations, both masters had discussed the alternative of turning back, either to Port Huron or to anchor in the protected waters of Thunder Bay. Captain Connelly deemed it safer to head into the seas, since turning a vessel under the existing conditions involved a period of time laboring in the trough of the seas while fighting to complete the turn. There was always the possibility that his light vessel might not have enough power to get out of the troughs and would quickly be overwhelmed. Captain Crawley, facing the same conditions and alternatives, apparently agreed.

Just before eleven o'clock, Captain Crawley called Captain Connelly again. But at the moment Captain Connelly was extremely busy. The *Townsend* had started to blow around, nearly broaching, falling off 22 degrees before she could be brought back on course with full left rudder and her engine laboring at full ahead.

"I'll call you back," promised Captain Connelly.

At five minutes after midnight Captain Connelly called Captain Crawley, who indicated that the *Daniel J. Morrell* had just been through a similar experience. Because both masters were busy trying to hold their vessels into the sea, the exchange was exceedingly brief. By now the wind, as reported by Captain Connelly, was northerly at sixty-five miles per hour with the seas "tremendous." By two o'clock on Wednesday morning, the wind had shifted to north-northeast and the seas had escalated to twenty-five feet. The *Townsend* was maintaining a continuous listening watch on radio-telephone channel 51, the calling and distress frequency. She was also taking solid water over the bow. Down below, as the *Townsend* pitched and rolled, the engineers were automatically reducing the engine revolutions when the propeller came out of the water. But although he tried several times during the early hours of the morning, when he estimated the *Morrell* to be about twenty miles ahead of him, Captain Connelly was unable to contact Captain Crawley. He concluded that the *Morrell* was having radio problems.

The *Daniel J. Morrell* and *Edward Y. Townsend* were not the only vessels experiencing difficulties on Lake Huron that night. Veteran sailors, including some who had weathered the "big blow" of 1913 and the Armistice Day storm of 1940, were quick to rate the present storm on a par with either of them, although admittedly more localized. The 1940 storm was concentrated more or less on Lake Michigan, but the 1913 blow was the result of a massive weather conspiracy that whipped all the lakes into a fury.

The motor vessel *Benson Ford*, which had anchored at

Bois Blanc Island in the Straits of Mackinac because of weather, heaved anchor shortly before nine o'clock that dreadful night and proceeded downbound into Lake Huron on the recommended steamer track. During one period of the night, while between Thunder Bay Island and the Lake Huron lightship, when the master estimated that the storm was at its greatest intensity, the wind, north by northeast, was fairly constant, a whole gale, at sixty knots with seas ranging to twenty-five feet with crests from 250 to 300 feet apart. The *Benson Ford* took considerable water over her stern and experienced some difficulty in handling in the following seas. Overhearing conversations between Captains Connelly and Crawley, the master concluded that both would be going to shelter at Thunder Bay. But reception was faulty, apparently, for neither vessel attempted the turning maneuver.

Captain Zernie Newman of the *Kinsman Independent* had passed the Lake Huron lightship earlier in the evening but experienced only light winds from the west. But by the time his coal-laden vessel reached the Harbor Beach area, the wind had moved to the north and was blowing at forty-five knots. Captain Newman tried to hold the *Kinsman Independent* into the wind, even after it had increased to fifty-five knots, but off Harbor Beach Light she "blew around" and lay in the punishing troughs for four minutes before the captain, with only 1800 horsepower at his disposal, could get her turned all the way around to flee back to shelter at Port Huron. During his battle with the seas, Captain Newman observed two "rollers" that he estimated to be twenty-eight feet in height.

The Canadian steamer *Howard L. Shaw*, also upbound, found the seas so high that her master, Captain L. D. Jones, estimated her "over the bottom" speed at only one or two knots. Finally, like the *Kinsman Independent*, she was blown around and, after two unsuccessful attempts to regain her heading into the seas, retreated to Port Huron for refuge.

Burdened with a full coal cargo, the self-unloading steamer *Fred A. Manske* had little choice but to keep heading into the seas. Almost blown around several times, she continued on simply because her master was reluctant to come about, due to the topside weight of her long unloading boom and the big "A" frame that supported it. In his opinion, the weight would possibly have proven fatal were the *Manske* to slide over into the troughs.

Like the *Kinsman Independent*, the *Robert Hobson* was loaded to her winter marks with coal. Although offering a lower profile to the wind in her loaded state, she was blown around four miles above Harbor Beach and proceeded back to Port Huron. Her master indicated that the winds were not surprising, but the seas were more than could be anticipated under the conditions.

Although the *Harry Coulby* had a 5000-horsepower steam plant, she was taking solid water over the bow when six miles above Port Sanilac. At this time her master was informed by radio telephone that other vessels ahead of him were experiencing even more violent weather and severe snow squalls in the Point Aux Barques area and were even then turning to run before the storm. He consequently turned his own vessel and made for Port Huron.

The U.S. Coast Guard Cutter *Acacia*, which had departed Harbor Beach shortly before eleven o'clock on Tuesday night, had two smaller Coast Guard craft scheduled for delivery at Sault Ste. Marie lashed to her deck. However, shortly after departure she was diverted to assist personnel on the ocean-going motor vessel *Nordmeer* after the salty's master had planted her on a rock off Thunder Bay Light. Shortly, however, the *Acacia* was released from the *Nordmeer* and proceeded on her way to the Soo. One hour and fifteen minutes later she was being so boisterously assaulted by the seas that one of the small craft on deck broke free of its lashings. The master, Lt. Commander Charles A. Millradt, made an attempt to reach shelter at Thunder Bay but was defeated by monstrous seas and blinding snow. Now, with the second small boat loose and receiving heavy damage he had little choice but to do as other, larger vessels were doing, beat a stormy path back to Port Huron.

The master of the *Henry Steinbrenner* was overheard remarking that he, too, turned to flee, but once his vessel fell off into the troughs it took eight terrifying minutes to get her all the way around.

Meanwhile, the *Daniel J. Morrell* and the *Edward Y. Townsend* were plugging onward. Both old, but typical of many vessels still earning their keep, they were forced by the wind and seas to steer one course to achieve another. In intermittent gales of snow they held as close to the prescribed course as possible, their aged hulls alternately hogging and sagging as the crests of twenty-five-foot seas lifted, turned, and dropped them. Graybeard combers exploded over their bows, spewing solid water the length of their spar decks as they pitched, rolled, and pounded. Snow squalls frequently made the forward and after ends islands unto themselves, each hidden from the other. Creaking, groaning, and emitting all the agonized sounds of tortured hulls, they pounded onward simply because by now there was no alternative. It was a night that tried men's souls and the skills of a past generation of shipbuilders.

Although built in different shipyards in 1906, the *Daniel J. Morrell* as hull Number 619 at West Bay City Shipbuilding Company and the *Edward Y. Townsend* as hull Number 515 at the Superior Shipbuilding Company, the two vessels were sister ships, alike as two peas in a pod. One peculiarity puzzled ship buffs. Although both were listed in Lloyd's Register as having keel lengths of 587 feet, the overall length varied in another directory; the *Morrell* was listed there as 600 feet in length, the *Townsend* as 602 feet. Did some prestige-conscious shipbuilder or owner fib a bit, or was a marine surveyor in error? It mattered little now, for in the uproarious seas that reigned on Lake Huron that night, both exhibited the same yawing, hogging, sagging, rolling, pitching, and pounding characteristics. And both were sixty-year veterans of just such seasonal freshwater traumas. The seasons were the usual four, but somehow the worst always came in November.

Watchman Dennis Hale, safely back in the good graces of the master and his shipmates, but still twenty-nine hours from his meeting with his ghostly, white-haired friend, finished his watch at eight o'clock that miserable Tuesday night. He made the windy walk aft to the galley later for hot coffee and whatever hearty fare steward Satlawa and porter Joe Mansem had to provide. After yarning with shipmates, Hale made the trip forward to his room, noting that quite a bit of water was sloshing up over the deck, the spume and froth of seas that had met the *Morrell* squarely on the bow and were now dissipating themselves on and among the hatch coamings the length of the spar deck. The wind appeared to be rising, judging from the whistling among the stays and railings of the forward cabins and pilot house. By now it was snowing steadily, a driving, blinding squall that made it difficult to open the eyes.

The warmth of his room, far forward in the fo'c'sle and next to the anchor windlass compartment, was welcome as Hale divested himself of his foul weather gear, read for a time, and at 9:30 P.M. climbed into his bunk. But in the tumult of the storm, which he judged had increased in its fury, sleep came slowly and fitfully. With monstrous seas slamming into the *Morrell*'s bluff bow, it was like trying to rest in a steel drum with an army of demons pounding on the outside. He awoke several times and on a couple of occasions could hear the anchors being bulled about by the seas, banging against the bow plates. In the windlass room, ropes, metal drums, cables, block, shovels, and all the associated working gear of the deck crew, hanging or stored, slid or went adrift, clanking and bumping as the vessel rolled, pitched, and pounded. Others quartered in the fo'c'sle were also trying to sleep amid the din: deckwatchman John Groh, watchman Albert Whoeme, Larry Davis, and Norman Bragg. So were deckhands Arthur Stojeck and John Cleary, Jr. Cleary was twenty, had been a sailor only two months, and was working on a temporary

permit. Hale was alone only because his roommate, watchman Clare Haley, had also missed the vessel at Lackawanna. Unlike Hale and Groh, he had made no attempt to
meet her elsewhere.

At about 2:00 A.M. on Wednesday morning, Dennis Hale
was awakened by a heavy-sounding bang, louder and quite
apart from the sound of the anchors pounding against the
bow. Shortly thereafter came another loud report, and with
this sound his books came tumbling down from a shelf to
bounce off his clothes chest and chair. Alarmed, he flipped
the switch of his bunk light but found it inoperable. At
almost the same instant the general alarm bells clanged.
He jumped up, grabbed a life jacket, and started down the
companionway to see what had gone wrong. Quick as he
was in reaching the heavy metal swinging door, Albert
Whoeme was there first, lifting the dogged-down handle
and peering out.

"Oh, my God," he cried, "Get your life jacket!"

A quick glance toward the *Morrell*'s stern revealed that
there were lights aft but that the deck appeared to have
been severed, the after section looming up higher than the
forward end.

Hale already had his life jacket but otherwise wore only
a pair of shorts. All lights on the forward end being out,
he fumbled his way back to his room, determined to find
and don his trousers and shoes. But in the complete darkness and with the *Morrell* rolling and yawing and the floor
cluttered with books, he could find neither trousers nor
shoes and settled instead for the only item of clothing he
could locate, his pea jacket.

He returned to the spar deck to find the forward crew

mustering around the life raft. Barefooted, he found that
the accumulated snow had turned to slush. Others were in
various stages of dress, none really prepared for the existing weather conditions. Getting aft to the lifeboats was out
of the question. Lifeboats, under the circumstances, were
only a psychological factor, for every shipmaster on Lake
Huron that night later stated that it would have been impossible to launch them.

The *Daniel J. Morrell* had eighteen hatches on twenty-
four-foot centers. The forward life raft, a pontoon-type device with slatted wooden floor and side sections, was located
on the spar deck between Number Three and Four hatches.
It could, if enough manpower were available, be thrown
over the side, but the most practical approach was simply
to sit in the raft and let it float off a foundering vessel.
This is where the forward crew gathered in the dark as one
of the strangest and most horrifying tragedies of the Great
Lakes unfolded.

Lashed by driving snow and freezing wind, soaked by the
spray and spume of seas breaking aboard, they watched in
awe as the after end of the *Morrell*, still with lights ablaze
and under power, charged ahead into the helpless, wallowing forward end, banging away as though all were well.
The scene was given an even more eerie, bizarre element
beyond the screeching of tortured steel and the shearing of
plates, as showers of sparks from severed electrical lines
and roaring steam from broken pipes added to the sights
and sounds, somehow terribly unreal there in the gale of
wind, snow, and water. And all the while the after end of
the vessel came charging and banging ahead, rending and

twisting whatever few shards of metal still joined the two halves.

That the forward end of the *Daniel J. Morrell* would sink and probably within a matter of minutes was never questioned by the shivering men hovering around the life raft . . . Captain Crawley; first mate Phillip Kapets; wheelsmen Henry Rischmiller, Stuart Campbell, Charles Fosbender; second mate Duncan MacLeod; watchmen Dennis Hale, Albert Whoeme, Norman Bragg, and Larry Davis; third mate Ernest Marcotta, and deckhands Arthur Stojek and young John Cleary.

The separation of the two sections was now complete, although the stern or after section was still under power, still bright with lights, and plowing insanely ahead to smash into the forward half. But at the point of the hull fracture, the after section, was now even higher than before, and the forward section seemed to be listing to starboard and was being turned by the wind and seas. The fracture, Dennis Hale estimated, was in the general area between hatches Eleven and Twelve.

There was little conversation beyond Captain Crawley's comment that a vessel had been sighted off the port bow and that another was astern of them. Wheelsman Fosbender had a flashlight and kept its beam darting about. Now the twisting action of the wind and huge seas was swinging the bow section to port; the pursuing after section hastened the action by constantly smashing into it. "Get on the raft and hold tight," said watchman Norman Bragg. Two who were already aboard were observed fumbling around in the dark for some rope to lash themselves to it. Even when the bow section had practically turned around and was almost parallel, the ragged end of the stern section kept crazily banging away. Finally the after end pushed the sinking forward section aside and continued its mad charge up the lake, lights bright and the propeller thrashing.

Now completely reversed, its gaping cargo hold open to the overwhelming rush of driving seas, the forward end began to sink. A huge sea, mounting the torn deck, swept the men and life raft, tumbling and turning, over the starboard side. Stunned by the impact and low water temperature, they thrashed around in the dark. When Dennis Hale surfaced, fortunately within a few strokes of the life raft, deckhands Stojek and Cleary were already aboard. Hale climbed on and helped the only other crewman within sight, wheelsman Charles Fosbender, over the side. Fosbender kept winking his flashlight at the disappearing stern section as though imploring those aboard to return for them. The four in the life raft were all that raging Lake Huron had spared.

Fosbender had finished his watch at midnight and had not yet retired when the lights went out and the general alarm sounded. He had grabbed a coat and his life jacket and consequently was the only one of the quartet fully clothed, although he was soaking wet from his swim to the life raft. Hale still wore only his shorts, pea jacket, and life jacket. Cleary, shivering uncontrollably, expressed a hope to be home for Christmas and wondered aloud how much of a chance they had to survive. "A lot better chance than those who didn't make it to this raft," Hale replied. Cleary wondered, too, how many children Hale had.

Hale immediately became preoccupied with the emergency storage box on the life raft. It held a signal pistol, six parachute flares, and six fixed amber flares. Other than a sea anchor and a can of storm oil, the spartan heritage of shipwrecked mariners, there was nothing. Hale planned to spread some of the storm oil over his frigid body in an attempt to preserve body heat, but one of the deckhands, after asking what it was, thoughtlessly tossed the can overboard.

Hale was under the impression when he went on deck immediately after the general alarm had sounded and he glanced toward the stern, that the lifeboat davits were swung out and the boats launched. He wondered to himself at the time how the after-end crew had accomplished this in so short a time, when he didn't even have time to find his trousers and shoes. But if the lifeboats had been launched, they would still have been in the area, with their own supply of flares and very probably flashlights. The four on the life raft saw nothing. Hale had noticed, however, that as the stern of the *Morrell* passed them and steamed away into the storm, that the after life raft, stored over the motor house at the vessel's fantail, was still in place.

Earlier, just before the two sections of the *Daniel J. Morrell* finally parted, someone had suggested sending up distress flares. But Captain Crawley had advised waiting until they were on the life raft and afloat. Now Hale went to carry out that suggestion. Two of the flares were lost over the side, dropped by numbed fingers. He fired off the first of the parachute flares, but after the third one the handle and barrel of the supposedly sturdy signal pistol parted. Thereafter he had to hold the parts together to fire off the remaining flares, which he spaced over a period of hours. The parachute flares functioned as designed, but their effectiveness was blunted by existing weather conditions—high winds, heavy snow squalls, and spume driven from the tops of breaking seas. So they passed the night, John Cleary, Arthur Stojek, Charles Fosbender and Dennis Hale, huddled in one end of the raft to share what little body heat was left, like four waifs of the street drawn close together for survival in an intensely hostile environment.

The *Edward Y. Townsend*, approximately twenty miles behind the *Daniel J. Morrell* when both vessels were off Harbor Beach, experienced the same atrocious conditions as did her sister ship. On Wednesday afternoon, water to a depth of forty-five inches was discovered in her cargo hold. This the master attributed to side ballast-tank leakage since the vessel left Lackawanna. Such leakage was considered normal, caused by damage inflicted by the unloading buckets and usually readily corrected by welding. On Thursday morning the *Townsend*, as instructed by the Cleveland office, stopped at Lime Island, in the lower St. Marys River, for bunker fuel. At this time Captain Connelly logically assumed that the *Daniel J. Morrell* had preceded him into the long river passage and attributed the radio silence as an indication of radio problems aboard the *Morrell*.

While his vessel was fueling, Captain Connelly received a report from his mates that loose rivets had been discovered in the spar dock plating, starboard side. Upon closer inspection, it was found that there was also a crack extending from the forward starboard corner of Number Ten hatch to and running beneath the deck strap, located between the hatches and sheerstrake, on the starboard side. Prior to this, Captain Connelly had not been aware of any structural damage. Normal working and springing had been experienced, but it was not considered excessive. The damage was reported to the Bethlehem marine department people, who in turn made the required report to the Coast Guard. Captain Connelly was instructed to continue on to Sault Ste. Marie, the Soo, at reduced speed. There the *Townsend* would undergo a close examination by Coast Guard inspectors.

Meanwhile, back on wild Lake Huron, in the gray haze of storm and capricious veils of snow fleeing like gypsies before the wind, the *Daniel J. Morrell*'s life raft, still swept by every sea, was being borne gradually shoreward by wind and wave. By now both John Cleary and Arthur Stojek had given up the fight to live. They died shortly after daybreak. Huddled under their bodies, Charles Fosbender and Dennis Hale experienced alternate periods of lucidity and fantasy. Fosbender, suffering greatly from a sinus condition, died at about four o'clock that afternoon. Now Dennis Hale was alone, his limbs numb and still drenched by every sea that broke over the tossing life raft.

Despite the absence of radio-telephone communication with the *Daniel J. Morrell*, operating personnel in the vessel's Cleveland office, disregarding the absence of required daily radio reports of position, waited an incredible thirty-six hours before notifying the Coast Guard at 12:15 P.M. on Thursday, November thirtieth, that the *Morrell* was overdue.

The Coast Guard's Rescue Coordination Center in Cleveland immediately initiated an all-ships broadcast, requesting all vessels to be on the lookout for the *Morrell*. The cutters *Mackinaw, Bramble,* and *Acacia* were immediately dispatched to the Lake Huron search area. Fixed-wing aircraft and helicopters from Detroit and Traverse City, Michigan, were also soon airborne and en route.

The fact that the *Daniel J. Morrell* had foundered became apparent earlier when crewmen of the *G. G. Post* sighted a body wearing one of the *Morrell's* life jackets eight miles off the Harbor Beach breakwater light. A Coast Guard vessel, notified by radio, had actually recovered the body five minutes before the *Morrell's* owners reported their vessel missing! Later, helicopters and cutters recovered seven more bodies in the same general area. They had been discovered by the steamer *G. A. Tomlinson*, whose skipper, Captain Joseph E. Fitch, reported them all sighted within a one-mile area. The *Morrell's* after life raft was found, unoccupied, but with one body trapped beneath it.

In the interim, Dennis Hale, huddled under the stiff bodies of his shipmates, with his feet and one hand frozen, experienced intervals of awareness and other interludes when his mind wandered. The life raft, meanwhile, was being carried closer to shore, its coloring making it difficult to spot from air or sea. The hours drifted by in pain and cold. His legs had long since ceased to have any feeling, and his hair was matted with ice.

It was in the afternoon of that fateful November thirtieth that Dennis Hale had two meetings with the ghostly stranger he still insists was his savior, encounters he would later omit in official testimony simply because he felt that nobody would believe him and that "it was a personal matter, beyond the ken of those who had never experienced such an ordeal." Once, he recalls it as early afternoon, in a period of complete wakefulness, hungry and thirsty, he was idly gnawing away at the icicles that had formed on the lapel of his pea jacket. Suddenly there was somebody else there with him, a rather elderly man with long white hair, a mustache, and heavy eyebrows and with a strange, milk-white complexion. Hale later couldn't recall how the man was dressed, simply because his electrifying appearance and penetrating eyes and demeanor commanded all attention. The ghostly old man sternly cautioned him against eating any more ice. Shortly thereafter Hale dropped off into another period of semiconsciousness, awakening later to again, subconsciously perhaps, chew away at the lengthening icicles. Again the ghostly, commanding figure appeared, sitting on the edge of the life raft. This time, in even sterner terms he berated Hale for his lapse of caution. "I told you not to eat the ice off your coat," said the old man with the milk-white complexion. "It will lower your body temperature and you'll die." In a few moments Hale drifted off again into the world of a man half alive, half dead. He was still semiconscious when, three miles below Huron City, Michigan, helicopter CG-1395 spotted the life raft and fluttered in alongside.

The helicopter crewmen, boarding the life raft and encountering what they presumed to be four frozen bodies, began to unstack them for transport to shore. But there on the bottom was Dennis Hale, covered with ice, trying weakly to wave one arm and smile a greeting. The helicopter quickly flew him to Harbor Beach Community Hospital.

There are always strange, conflicting emotions and coincidental circumstances associated with major disasters, and such was the case with the often itinerant fraternity of men whose fellowship had been part of the *Daniel J. Morrell* through the season of 1966. When Huron County deputy sheriffs telephoned Bertha Hale in Ashtabula to tell her that her husband was the only survivor of a shipwreck and would apparently fully recover, Mrs. Hale had not yet been apprised of the *Morrell*'s loss. Back in Buffalo, the two firemen who had paid off as soon as the vessel tied up to the Lackawanna ore dock were congratulating themselves on their rare sense of intuition and toasting that rare gift with some frequency. Happy, too, was deckhand Mark Petroff, of Erie, Pennsylvania. He, too, left the vessel at Lackawanna, but his sense of relief was tempered with grief for his lost shipmates. Milo Becker, the oiler called home by family illness, was equally distraught.

Up in Sault Ste. Marie, in War Memorial Hospital, sixty-one-year-old Hjaimer Edwards gloomily perused the casualty list, noting many old friends now lost. Edwards had once been a chief steward in the old Hutchinson fleet. But the company ceased operations, and Edwards, without seniority, had been forced to work as a porter for other vessel operators. He was porter on the *Daniel J. Morrell* but had been taken ill and left the ore-laden downbound vessel at the Soo locks on Thanksgiving Day.

Strangely, the compilation of dead and missing at Harbor Beach brought unexpected good news to thirteen-year-old Patricia Haley. Her father, Clare G. Haley, the man who missed the boat at Lackawanna and was Dennis Hale's roommate, was among the names on the preliminary list of men lost with the *Morrell*. For ten years, ever since her parents had been divorced, Patricia had wondered where her father was and what he was doing. She and her mother, now Mrs. Betty Pressnell, set out for Harbor Beach, but before they got there learned that the final death list deleted the name of Clare G. Haley. He, like Hjaimer Edwards, left the ship only days before it foundered. The father and daughter subsequently communicated by phone, a conversation that inspired Patricia to exclaim, "This is the most wonderful day of my life!"

In Cleveland, Ray Rockey, manager of Jim's Steak House, hard by the Cuyahoga River at Collision Bend, mourned for the loss of his good friend, Captain Arthur Crawley. The captain, when his vessel was bound upriver to the ore docks, would sometimes flash the big searchlight at the restaurant and, if he intended later to return for a meal, would give the whistle a brief but special blast.

At St. Clair, Michigan, about the time the *Morrell*'s victims were being tabulated, Jan Fosbender was receiving a letter from her husband, wheelsman Charles Fosbender, one of Dennis Hale's life raft companions. He had posted it with the mail boat that came alongside in the Detroit River. "If luck holds with us, it will be our last trip," wrote Fosbender. It was.

Meanwhile, following official orders, Captain Connelly steamed the *Edward Y. Townsend* slowly up the St. Marys River to dock at Sault St. Marie. There, boarding Coast Guard inspectors conducted a preliminary survey of the vessel, discovering spar deck cracks and other such evidence of excessive strain and metal failure that would justify the vessel being "arrested," her sailing papers revoked. Fractures, some of them old, were found in the double-bottom tanks as well as other stress distortions, corrosion, and evidence of loosened rivets, the result of recent working and springing under stress of weather. The Coast Guard ordered the *Townsend* to drydock for further internal and external inspection and necessary repairs. A permit to proceed to the location of a drydock was issued, authorizing the vessel to be towed, unmanned.[1] As a matter of record she spent the winter at the Soo, in a winter layup status.

It was a traumatic situation for the Coast Guard, charged with the necessary periodic inspection of existing vessels, ascertaining maintenance and seaworthiness. The service's Marine Board of Investigation that subsequently convened was more than aware that the average age of the Great Lakes bulk carrier fleet was about forty-five years, with more vessels in the fifty- to sixty-year age group than any other ten-year period. These vessels, it was also known, were constructed of a type of steel that had not been used since 1948. This pre-1948 steel generally had a high transition temperature and was therefore susceptible to brittle fracture. While corrosion in the fresh water of the Great Lakes is minimal, the board recognized that metal fatigue,

[1] The *Edward Y. Townsend* never carried another Great Lakes cargo. Practically at the end of her career in any event, she was sold on the foreign scrap market. Ironically, she, like the *Daniel J. Morrell,* broke in half and foundered in the Atlantic while being towed to Santander, Spain. It is significant that of a dozen vessels sold abroad for scrap in the decade beginning in 1960, eight failed to reach their destinations. The *Arcturus, Perseus, W. Wayne Hancock, North American, Mohawk Deer, Laketon,* and *Edward Y. Townsend* all foundered, while the *Fayette Brown* stranded on Anticosti Island.

the result of repeated years of working, springing, and twisting in the seas, can and did result in local structural deterioration in the form of fatigue cracks.

If the Marine Board of Investigation convened to investigate the loss of the *Daniel J. Morrell* was a little sensitive to the situation, it might be recalled that it had only been eight years, again in stormy November, when the *Carl D. Bradley* suffered catastrophic hull failure in Lake Michigan, resulting in the loss of the vessel and all but two of her crew. At the time, lake seamen and their unions had been highly critical of both the Coast Guard and vessel operators. Significantly, the *Carl D. Bradley* had been built in 1927, twenty-one years after the *Daniel J. Morrell* and the *Edward Y. Townsend.* Nor was it considered pertinent that some of the other vessels on Lake Huron the night the *Morrell* foundered were also somewhat advanced in years. The *Howard L. Shaw* had been laid down in 1900, the *Kinsman Independent* and *Henry Steinbrenner* in 1907, and the *Fred A. Manske* in 1909. The *Benson Ford* dated back to 1924, the *Robert L. Hobson* to 1926, and the *Harry Coulby* was built in 1927. It was a situation pregnant with ominous possibilities, and obviously the Coast Guard had to take constructive action even though it entailed radical procedures.

Commandant of the U.S. Coast Guard Admiral Willard J. Smith contracted with Ocean Systems, Incorporated, to locate, identify, and take television pictures of the wreckage of the *Daniel J. Morrell* and retrieve sections of metal. The wayward bow section, brushed aside by the charging stern section, was not located, but aircraft from the naval air station, equipped with magnetic detection devices, located the sunken stern. Divers working from the cutter *Bramble* were able positively to identify the severed stern and conducted an underwater survey that continued through January and into February.

The stern section was resting in 210 feet of water, had settled appreciably in the mud, and had a slight port list. Piles of mud on the spar deck adjacent to the hull break indicated that this area had plowed into the bottom first. Divers also found that the primary crack in the deck and sheerstrake on the starboard side occurred at web frame 107. This frame was located adjacent to and even with the forward coaming of Number Eleven hatch. The fracture line on the deck, starboard, ran through a transverse row of rivet holes to the hatch coaming. The crack in the starboard sheerstrake was basically vertical and passed from rivet hole to rivet hole. The location of the break on the port side was between hatches Eleven and Twelve, at about frame 113. The break in the deck stringer followed a transverse row of rivets. The crack in the sheerstrake, port side, was vertical and did not occur in the area of rivets. The port deck seam strap cracked through a line of rivets about six inches forward of the break in the deck stringer. All underdeck longitudinals showed evidence of severe distortions, some doubled back upon themselves. Deck and side plating showed evidence of extreme bending, some as much as 180 degrees from the original. The deck stringer, starboard side, had been bent down to an angle of about ninety degrees. This section was recovered for analysis, as was a large section of the sheerstrake, starboard, with a section of the seam strap and "L" strake.

The *Daniel J. Morrell*'s hatches and coal bunker were

found open with hatch covers strewn about the area of the hull. Many hatch clamps had been broken. Divers found both the port and starboard lifeboat davits in the cranked-in position, the starboard lifeboat still attached to the boat falls, its cover still in place. The port lifeboat was missing, presumably because the after mast had toppled and had fallen in the same confined area, probably crushing its air tanks and the boat itself. In pursuit of facts, the Coast Guard submitted the recovered steel hull parts for analysis to the Battelle Memorial Institute, in Columbus, Ohio.

The analysis and study indicated a brittle fracture typical of many prior ship fractures in pre-1948 steel, a fracture that occurred in the spar deck and sheerstrake on the starboard side at frame 107. The source of the fracture in the deck plate was not contained in the sections recovered. However, the chevron pattern in the fracture indicated that it initiated inboard of the retrieved sample. The fracture in the sheerstrake at frame 107 began at the third rivet hole below the upper edge. However, the minimal deterioration of steel in fresh water was again evident in the examination. The original thickness of the steel deck and sheerstrake was .980 inches. The average thickness of the retrieved metal was .965 inches, a corrosion of less than 2 per cent over a period of sixty years.

The conclusion of the Marine Board of Investigation, therefore, was that the casualty was caused by a structural failure in the hull girder, amidships, which resulted in the break-up of the vessel and that the cause of the structural failure was a combination of factors that produced successive brittle fractures. These factors were: a high stress load due to extremely heavy weather conditions; a notch-sensitive steel (susceptible to fracture), which could have produced notches in a rivet hole; a welded plate insert on the inboard edge of the auxiliary stringer at Number Eleven hatch, starboard side; or possibly recently incurred bucket damage to the inboard edge of the auxiliary stringer in the vicinity of frame 107, starboard side; and a water temperature of 33 degrees, Fahrenheit, which was below the nil ductility temperature of the steel. Another factor considered in the conclusion was the free surface water in cargo holds Two and Three, which might have caused an unusual strain to an already weakened area as the result of dynamic forces of shifting weight due to pitching, rolling, pounding and twisting as the bow of the vessel was blown around.

It was also concluded that any ballasted vessel of a design similar to that of the *Daniel J. Morrell* would suffer severe stresses and strains in sea conditions such as were present on that terrible night, particularly if such a vessel remained in or at an angle to the troughs of the seas for any length of time. The evaluation was predicated upon the fact that a 600-foot vessel at an angle of approximately thirty degrees to seas having crests 250 to 300 feet apart would suffer severe hogging, sagging, and twisting stresses. The findings also noted that cracks on the *Edward Y. Townsend* were in the same general deck area and that both vessels were headed into the wind and sea under the same weather and sea conditions.

Statistics and official findings find little sympathy among those most intimately affected, mostly sailors and the families of shipwreck victims. Neither brings back lost lives.

A review of the required five-year Coast Guard sight-and-survey inspections was obviously a matter of keen interest. During November and December 1960, while the *Daniel J. Morrell* was in drydock in Ashtabula, Ohio, approximately 9500 shell rivets and thirteen shell plates were replaced. There were numerous other internal repairs and replacements. All work was inspected and tested satisfactorily.

The next drydocking was in February of 1966, when two hull inspectors and one boiler inspector went over the vessel thoroughly. As a result of this inspection, three shell plates were replaced as well as repairs made to eleven bilge brackets and three web floors. The remainder of the hull plating appeared to be in good condition. Approximately fifty shell rivets were also required to be replaced by the inspection party. In eight of the vessel's side and double bottom tanks, the inspectors required numerous routine repairs, such as the refastening of stiffeners and brackets and the repairing of cracked welds in brackets and angles. In addition, numerous repairs were completed in the cargo holds to mend bucket damage inflicted while unloading. The senior hull inspector signed the drydock examination book: "In my opinion the vessel is fit for the service and route specified." That, too, was the judgment and verdict of the boiler inspector.

At the first of a series of official Coast Guard hearings, the testimony of several former officers and crewmen was often conflicting. The board of inquiry, anxious to get all the testimony possible, traveled to cities where the former officers or crewmen lived or worked. Survivor Dennis Hale, who had been transferred to Ashtabula General Hospital in his home town, told the board that at layup time the previous fall he saw "at least a thousand rivets marked with white paint, indicating they needed repair." He recalled, too, that in the spring fitout first mate Phillip Kapets had complained that requested winter repairs had not been made. Hale also remembered a conversation he had with Harvey Hays of Wesleyville, Pennsylvania, a crewman on the *Morrell* in 1965. Hays, said Hale, told him that leaks in the cargo hold were so bad they washed off the paint Hays was using to mark them. Another former crewman who served on the vessel both in 1964 and 1965 testified that it was in generally sound condition. In Ogdensburg, New York, Frank Bryan, another former *Morrell* crew member, commented on many leaking rivets and accumulations of water in the side tanks. A former third mate of the *Morrell*, Thomas Burns, told the board that "seepage is not uncommon, particularly in the older lake boats."

Coast Guard Lt. Leonard E. Engstrum, the inspector who the previous February had certified that the *Daniel J. Morrell* was "fit for service on the route specified," testified that "there had been a lot of maintenance and replacement parts but she was in better condition than most vessels of that age."

Captain William L. Hull, second mate on the *Morrell* in 1956 and master from July of 1964 until he turned the vessel over to Captain Crawley in August of 1966, contradicted much of the previous testimony as to the vessel's deteriorated condition. He insisted that virtually all repairs requested to be made during the 1965–1966 winter were completed and that repairs to bottom or side tanks were made as they became necessary during the 1966 shipping season. He said that two of the tanks continued to leak, but not to a significant degree.

Lynwood C. Harivel, fleet engineer for the Bethlehem-operated steamer, testified that he was aboard the *Morrell* before she left Lackawanna that fateful Sunday night and that "there was nothing wrong with the ship." But more significantly, he reported that there was no emergency radio equipment on board, nor was such required by Coast Guard regulations. It was brought out that, like others in the Great Lakes fleet, regular radio-telephone gear on the bridge at the forward end of the vessel got its only power from equipment in the stern. Thus, when a vessel broke in two the radio was inoperable. In a catastrophic turn of events such as the *Morrell*'s complete hull failure, the ship's crew would be unable to send a distress call.

Before and while the general condition and last hours of the *Daniel J. Morrell* were under scrutiny, lawsuits filed by families of the victims were piling up, all of them contending that the vessel was unseaworthy.[2] Survivor Dennis Hale also sought damages for his suffering and subsequent disability.

During testimony before the investigative board, attorneys representing relatives and maritime unions tried to pin down rumors that the *Morrell*'s engine and boilers were something less than in seaworthy condition. But the rumors were not substantiated by credible testimony; they

[2] Largely because of the findings contained in the National Transportation Safety Board report, the Bethlehem Steel Corporation, in a pretrial settlement, agreed to pay $2,750,000 to the claimants, all family survivors of men lost when the *Daniel J. Morrell* went down. The settlement, announced on October 7, 1970, was one of the largest in maritime history.

were ruled hearsay, and that included a copy of a letter coalpasser Leon Truman of Toledo had mailed to his wife on November 6th. Wrote Truman, "The fog lifted about 7 A.M. this morning so we could get into the dock. Two more tubes blew in the boiler. This old boat is just about had it."

With unpleasant memories of the *Carl D. Bradley* still very much a haunting reality, and existing inspection and safety standards again being questioned, the Coast Guard continued to conduct what was probably the most extensive and, to this point, revolutionary investigation of any Great Lakes shipwreck. But investigations never bring back lives or resurrect a vanished steamer. They can only determine the probable causes of a disaster, and, in the case of the *Daniel J. Morrell*, the causes were beyond a reasonable doubt. An investigation can, however, point up a need for changes and procedures that may prevent repetitions. The Coast Guard inquiry did indeed bring about changes by recommendation. And with the shipping industry "under the microscope," so to speak, recommendations were quickly transposed into constructive action.

It had long been recognized that in really severe weather, such as was encountered on Lake Huron that dreadful night, lifeboats were literally useless because they could not be launched. They were merely psychological factors, nothing more. In any event, when a vessel broke in two, they were available only to the after-end crew. The long-standard pontoon-type life rafts were abandoned in favor of self-inflating life rafts with canopies to shelter crews from the elements. Battery-powered emergency radios were made standard equipment in pilot houses, an assurance that a Mayday message could still be sent even after total hull failure such as was suffered by the *Morrell.* Dual-powered emergency alarms also quickly became standard equipment.

As was expected, the Marine Board of Investigation strongly urged special examination of the hull structures of all Great Lakes vessels built prior to 1948, when the new ship steel specifications were adopted. As a result of this recommendation, many such vessels subsequently went to the shipbreakers, their owners reluctant to expend large sums of money for reconstruction and structural rein-forcement on steamers whose carrying capacities rendered profits marginal at best.

When the National Transportation Safety Board, under whose auspices the Marine Board of Investigation func-tioned, eventually compiled its thirty-four page "Findings of Fact" report, it was probably responsible for more con-structional, operational, and procedural changes than any other document in Great Lakes history. But it was too late, far too late, for Captain Arthur I. Crawley, wheelsman Charles Fosbender, chief engineer John Schmidt, fireman Arthur Fargo, coalpasser Leon Truman, and twenty-three of their shipmates. And it was of little help to the lone survivor, watchman Dennis Hale. Although eternally grate-ful for being alive, he went through a long period of dis-ability because of his frozen feet—the result of long im-mersion in the flooded life raft and exposure to freezing wind and seas—requiring three operations and prolonged therapy treatment.

Today, done with sailing and working as a machine oper-ator, Hale has his own special philosophy about why he was spared. "Call it fate or an act of God or whatever you will," he says. "Certainly God was watching over me, but I can't forget that strange visitor I had during those final, critical hours on the life raft. How could you, with that haunting, compelling, milk-white face and that flowing white hair, mustache, and bushy eyebrows. Who knows what the end would have been had I ignored his instructions. Some will call it fatigue-inspired imagination, hallucinations, or whatever, but I know he was real because I was there!"

12

·
·
·
·

⚓

A Bell Tolls Twenty-Nine
for "Big *Fitz*"

It figured that even before she made her freshwater debut in a rousing and spectacular side launching at River Rouge, Michigan, that the *Edmund Fitzgerald* would be dubbed "Big *Fitz*" by the marine fraternity. For at the moment of her christening and launch on June 8, 1958, she was the largest Great Lakes vessel afloat, boasting an overall length of 729 feet, a 75-foot beam, and a lusty midsummer draft capacity of 25,891 gross tons. By any sailor's standards she was a big, beamy beauty.

But it figured, too, that she would lose this distinction when the new longer and wider Poe Lock opened at the Soo eleven years later and a new generation or "class" of vessels would be forthcoming—thundering big steamers like the 858-foot *Roger Blough* and the 1000-foot *Stewart J.*

Cort, both with 105-foot beams and an insatiable appetite for iron ore cargoes.[1]

Inevitably and understandably, the "Big" in "Big *Fitz*" was surreptitiously, almost automatically, dropped. But to those who knew her intimately she remained their beloved *Fitz,* still almost a new boat by Great Lakes longevity tables.

Although owned by the Northwestern Mutual Life Insurance Company and named for Edmund Fitzgerald, who became its chairman of the board a month before the ship was christened, the new steamer was under long-term charter to Cleveland's Oglebay Norton Company, and thereafter the vessel's manifold affairs were efficiently managed by that company's Columbia Transportation Division. Oglebay Norton has long been preeminent in lake shipping, mining, and the development and processing of raw materials.

For all of her life, which was destined to be seventeen years, the *Fitz*'s days at sea or in port were managed by highly competent and experienced officers. She was flagship of the Columbia fleet, and duty aboard the *Fitz* was a prized assignment that went only to the best and most deserving, usually those with long years of service.

The honor of "bringing out" the *Fitz* after she was commissioned in September of 1958 went to Captain Bert Lambert, a senior skipper making his "last hurrah" as a shipmaster before scheduled retirement at the end of the shipping season.

1 Following the *Roger Blough* and *Stewart J. Cort* came other new vessels, such as the *James R. Barker,* designed to take advantage of the 1000-foot length and 105-foot beam limitation of the new Poe Lock. Others are abuilding or on the drawing boards. Several existing vessels, such as the *John Sherwin, Arthur M. Anderson, Charles M. Beeghly,* and several units of the U.S. Steel Corporation fleet have been lengthened.

Appointed master at the beginning of the 1959 season was Captain Newman C. "Joe" Larsen, a veteran shipmaster with impeccable credentials. When Captain Larsen retired at the end of the 1965 shipping season, he was succeeded by the doughty and effervescent Peter Pulcer, an articulate and thoroughly qualified man who, like his predecessor, had an enviable record as a capable and cautious shipmaster. Because he commanded the flagship, he often humorously referred to himself as the "Commodore" of the Columbia fleet.

When Captain Pulcer retired at the end of the 1971 season, Captain Ernest M. McSorley, a sailor for forty-four years, replaced him. Like the others, Captain McSorley, a quiet, unassuming man, came up the long, slow, and hard way. Beginning with Columbia in 1938 as a wheelsman and progressing through the usual third, second, and first mate experience ranks, he finally gained command of the *Carrollton* in 1951.

Columbia has always operated what is probably the most diversified fleet on the Great Lakes. In addition to the usual straight-deck coal, stone, iron ore, and grain carriers, they have also floated a considerable armada of smaller vessels, including self-unloaders and crane boats, the latter hauling everything from bulk chemicals to pig iron, wire, and scrap. Most Columbia skippers have made it to the larger, more prestigious vessels only after long apprenticeships aboard smaller and older boats.

After his season on the *Carrollton*, Captain McSorley served as master on the *William E. Stifel* and *Ben E. Tate*. He spent 1955 on the *Harry T. Ewig* and 1956 on the *Robert J. Paisley*, before beginning a two-year stint on the

J. R. Sensibar. Next came three years on the *W. W. Hollo-way,* before returning for three more seasons on the *J. R. Sensibar.* Then the *Joseph H. Frantz* was his command for four years before moving up to the larger *Armco* in 1970.

Time has a habit of bringing a patient man his just rewards and with the well-earned retirement of Peter Pulcer late in 1971, Ernest McSorley was elevated to command of the *Fitz.*

Unlike captains, who move readily from command to command, chief engineers, by the very nature of their profession, are very likely to become wedded to their machinery. The complicated power plants that drive large vessels have their individual characteristics, demands, and temperaments. Owners, therefore, are often prone to keep a man with the machinery whose moods and needs he has come to know intimately. Consequently, the big 7500-horsepower twin steam turbines that drove the *Fitz* knew only two chief engineers over the years—Wendle Freeman, who "brought her out," and George Holl, who succeeded him in 1971. During the winter of 1971–1972 the ship's original coal-fired boilers had been replaced with oil-fired equipment.

In the early afternoon of November 9, 1975, a warm and sunny day belied the usual weather conditions for Duluth-Superior for that time of year. On area courses, golfers were getting in what might prove to be the final rounds of 1975. The *Fitz* was topping off a cargo of 26,116 tons of taconite pellets at the Burlington Northern Dock in Superior. The loading was supervised by first mate John H. "Jack" McCarthy, who followed a time-proven formula for the weight distribution of the ore pellets. When the last charge came rattling down the chute, the deck crew set about closing the hatches. The hatch crane bell clanging, they positioned the last of the one-piece hatch covers—solid, exceedingly heavy steel plates—and began snapping on the many securing clamps.

It was definitely not average November weather for the western end of Lake Superior. But the periodic weather report received on the radio-telephone in the *Fitz's* pilot house was more typical of the month. Captain McSorley, as doubtless did other shipmasters, glumly perused the coded dispatch, which forecast strong, gale-force northeast winds, spawned by a low pressure system originating in Kansas. The massive disturbance increased its circulation and intensity as it progressed northeastward, typified by falling barometric pressure as it curved back in a counter-clockwise track, boiling over eastern Lake Superior. This was certainly more like November. Unfortunately, although its subsequent character could not then be predicted, it was to develop into what the National Oceanic and Atmospheric Administration was later to term the Great Lakes "Storm of the Year."

At approximately 2:30 the *Fitz* departed Duluth-Superior. Part of the deck crew snapped shut the very last hatch cover clamps, and others began hosing down the deck, clearing off stray pellets and ore dust. It was a routine as familiar as chipping and painting.

Something like two hours and a half after the *Fitz* departed her loading dock, she overtook the *Arthur M. Anderson*, which had loaded pellets at Two Harbors, Minnesota, thirty-five miles north of Duluth. The *Anderson's* cargo was destined for Gary, Indiana; the *Fitz's* 26,116 tons for the Zug Island steel-making complex on the Detroit River. (In 1973 the American Bureau of Shipping and the United States Coast Guard had determined that vessels of the *Fitz*'s class, with specific modifications, were thoroughly capable of carrying larger cargoes and authorized an adjustment of the Plimsoil lines, permitting deeper loading. But the current burden of the *Fitz* was still below her new rated capacity.)

The *Fitz*, having a bit more speed than the *Anderson*, gradually pulled away. But Captain McSorley and Captain Jesse B. "Bernie" Cooper of the *Anderson*, conferring by radio, agreed that the deteriorating weather justified taking the "north shore" route, in the lee of the Canadian mainland, rather than following the normal, mid-lake downbound course. It is a somewhat longer steamer track but an infinitely easier one in bad weather.

Weather conditions, beginning with rain, deteriorated during the evening as both vessels crawled past Rock of Ages Light, Siskiwit Bay, and the long bulk of Isle Royale, steering always a curving course that would keep them well off the Slate Islands before rounding more sharply to starboard to keep them a respectable distance off Otter Head. By midnight the distance separating them ranged from ten to fifteen miles, and now the driving rain was mixed with snow.

The *Fitz* was one of forty-five Great Lakes vessels enlisted in a vast weather reporting system supervised by William Kennedy, port meteorological officer at the United States Weather Bureau in Cleveland. Ship reports every six hours, and similar reports from forty Coast Guard stations every two hours, provided up-to-the-minute weather status determinations on which official weather reports were issued.

At about midnight, November 9th, when both vessels were being hammered by great winds pounding down over Nipigon Bay and Jackfish Bay from the Canadian mainland, the *Fitz*, call letters FTZ, sent in a report that she, and obviously the *Anderson*, were encountering high seas, intermittent heavy rain, snow flurries, and forty-two-knot winds, northeast by north. However, both vessels continued on at full speed, taking considerable spray but no green water. The *Fitz* was slightly closer to the Canadian shore than the *Anderson*.

Ironically, partly because of the *Fitz*'s weather report and others from ships and shore stations, at 1:00 A.M. a heavy storm warning was issued by radio. Both vessels received the warning.

Off Heron Bay the two ships hauled to starboard to pass well off Otter Head. The course planned by both skippers would keep them about two and one-half miles off the west side of Michipicoten Island. The wind was howling vengefully, ranging between fifty to sixty knots with occasional gusts near seventy, putting green water over the *Anderson*'s deck. At this time the *Fitz* was between seven and ten miles ahead of the *Anderson*.

The *Fitz* continued on the planned course, but Captain Cooper of the *Anderson*, quite a student of weather, knew from experience and forecasts that a change in the wind direction could come at any time. Consequently he wanted more distance between his vessel and Michipicoten Island and so directed the helmsman. The *Fitz*, however, would be beyond Michipicoten before the anticipated change.

"It was blowing a real gagger," recalled Captain Cooper.

The normal north shore or bad-weather course dictates an angling approach to the area between Michipicoten Island and Caribou Island. There are two long-known hazards in this passage. First, below Michipicoten there is a fifteen-fathom area called Chummy Bank. More significantly, a roughly defined six-fathom or thirty-six-foot shoal extends out northerly from Caribou Island. The shoal area, in Canadian water, was last charted in 1919. And, also of great importance, there are other shoal areas, slightly off the normal steamer tracks, with least depths of thirty feet.

Captain Cooper chose not to approach the passage on the normal angle but, instead, hauled around to starboard, or southwest, for a spell before hauling to port again to make the passage head-on to the seas and midway between Michipicoten and Caribou, coincidentally about midway between Chummy Bank and the shoals north of Caribou, the most respected and feared of which was known as the North Bank. The seas in those shoal waters, he later explained, can become tremendous and "break crazy." But once safely between the islands, it's another sharp starboard haul and a straight shot to the shelter of Whitefish Bay. The *Anderson's* maneuver widened the gap between the vessels to seventeen miles.

Although not visually observable through rain and intermittent snow, the *Fitz* was a steady target on the *Anderson's* radar, and the two masters were in frequent radio communication.

At one point, probably about three o'clock on the afternoon of the 10th, Captain McSorley stated that the seas were "tremendous, the worst I have ever seen."

"The way the seas were running down there, it must have been a hell of a sea," Captain Cooper later related.

It is significant to note at this time that the direction-finding radio beacon at Whitefish Point Light was inoperable, or at best functioning inconsistently. Even more importantly to the *Fitz*, the radio beacon at Caribou Island was also out of order and silent. Captain McSorley had been asking other vessels if the Whitefish Point signal was operating, for he apparently couldn't receive it.

The *Anderson*, at this point, as Captain Cooper stated, was "taking a lacing, heading right into it and taking water on both sides."

But what appalled and frightened Captain Cooper and first mate Morgan Clark as they observed the *Fitz*'s plot on radar, was the course Captain McSorley had chosen to make the passage between Michipicoten and Caribou Island. He was, in their estimation, too close, far too close, to the six-fathom or thirty-six-foot shoal area. They watched the *Fitz* ease over the shoal area, but then the tremendous seas obscured everything and only "sea return" registered on the radar—seas were so high they interfered with the radar beams. However, radio contact was maintained.

As Captain Cooper later reported to his superiors in the United States Steel Corporation fleet, "I swear he went in there . . . in fact, we were talking about it. We were concerned that he was in too close, that he was going to hit that shoal off Caribou. I mean, God, he was about three miles off the beacon." And the beacon Captain Cooper referred to was Caribou Island Light, on the far or southerly end of the island.

To a vessel drawing in the neighborhood of twenty-seven feet, the thirty-six-foot shoals would probably present no problem in a flat calm sea. But the *Fitz*, like the *Anderson*, was pounding in twenty- to thirty-foot seas, dropping down precipitously and constantly hogging and sagging as her hull support from the seas varied from second to second.

At 3:30 P.M. Captain McSorley called Captain Cooper, reporting that the *Fitz* had cracked off a couple of vent pipes, had lost her fence (railing), and was taking on a list.

"I am taking water down the vent pipes," he reported. "Will you stick around by me until we get down?"

Captain Cooper replied in the affirmative and asked if the *Fitz*'s pumps were working.

"Yes, both of them," replied Captain McSorley.

Since the *Fitz* was the faster boat, her captain stated that he would check his vessel down to allow the *Anderson* to close the gap between them.

Periodically during the late afternoon and early evening, both Captain Cooper and mate Morgan Clark were in radio contact with Captain McSorley. On each occasion he reported that conditions were about the same.

While Captain Cooper was out of the pilot house for a few moments, Captain McSorley called, reporting that one radar set was out, the other undependable, and that he would appreciate the *Anderson* giving him bearings. First mate Clark advised him of his current position, fifteen miles north of the highlands of Crisp Point.

"I am holding my own," said Captain McSorley at ten minutes after seven. "We are going along like an old shoe. No problems at all."

The *Anderson*, meanwhile, had closed to within nine miles. But it was snowing hard and sea return on the radar still blanked out the *Fitz*.

To both Captain Cooper and first mate Clark the remarks of Captain McSorley seemed calm, measured, and confident, with no hint of strain or worry.

But on the saltwater vessel *Avorfors*, coming out of Whitefish Bay, the pilot, Captain Cedric Woodard, got a contrasting impression. He was a friend of Captain McSorley and thoroughly familiar with McSorley's voice. Woodard called the *Fitz* and asked a strange voice to let him speak to the captain.

"This is the captain," said McSorley.

"I didn't recognize him," said Woodard. "But then, he might have had a cold or was just weary."

Again, at shortly after 7:10 P.M., although the *Fitz*'s blip was not visible on radar, mate Clark picked up a radar image of the saltwater vessel *Nanfri*, also coming out of Whitefish Bay, and advised the *Fitz* by radio. This message was acknowledged. Clark busied himself trying to adjust the radar to pick up the blip of the *Fitz*, but without success. The *Nanfri* was called by radio and asked if they saw any lights or radar image of the *Fitz*. The pilot of the *Nanfri*, Captain Jacovetti, responded in the negative.

Captain Cooper then called the *William Clay Ford*, anchored in Whitefish Bay, to ascertain if the *Fitz* had possibly reached the same refuge. Again, the answer was in the negative. Neither had a neighboring steamer, the *Hilda Marjanne*, seen the *Fitz*.

Another salty, the 709-foot *Benfri*, was also upbound.

The pilot, Captain Robert O'Brien, heard the *Anderson* calling the *Fitz* and checked his own radar. There was no blip for the *Fitz*. The *Fitz* had disappeared!

Captain Cooper, extremely apprehensive, contacted Coast Guard Soo Control, relaying his fears and the last known position of the missing vessel. Soo Control immediately began a radio check of vessels known to be in the area and asked Captain Cooper if he would turn and retrace his track to the last known position of the *Fitz*.

But Captain Cooper was already in the process of doing just that. He turned the *Anderson* near Parisienne Island, in Whitefish Bay, and pounded back along his track, finding not a trace of the *Fitz* or her people. During the hunt, seas built up by the tremendous wind whistling out over Coppermine Point, Cape Gargantua, and Batchawana Bay smashed the *Anderson*'s starboard lifeboat and carried away deck gear.

The saltwater vessels also mounted watches, and at Whitefish Bay masters of other vessels, responding to word of a fellow mariner in distress, got their vessels underway. Among them was the *William Clay Ford*, although she was light and in ballast. Crew members volunteered for watches on the exposed decks and rigging, looking for any sign of the *Fitz* or wreckage. They saw nothing.

Soo Control, meanwhile, alerted the Coast Guard Rescue Coordination Center in Cleveland, advising that uncertainty existed as to the fate of the steamer *Edmund Fitzgerald*, which had apparently dropped from the face of the earth.

Search aircraft from the Coast Guard air station at Traverse City, Michigan, were immediately dispatched, and

The ill-fated *Daniel J. Morrell,* photographed going about her routine duties on the St. Clair River shortly before her final voyage.

Compatriots in a subsequent grim drama on Lake Huron, the *Edward Y. Townsend,* center, and the *Daniel J. Morrell,* right, are anchored with a sister vessel, the *Bethlehem,* behind the Cleveland breakwall during a strike of steelworkers.

Plain Dealer *photo by Ray Matjasic*

Port Huron Times Herald *photo*
Still sheltered under the bodies of his dead shipmates, Dennis Hale is about to be rescued by a Coast Guard helicopter.

Diver, operating from the Coast Guard cutter *Bramble,* about to descend to the sunken steamer *Daniel J. Morrell.*

U.S. Coast Guard photo

Half-ton vertical section from the hull of the sunken steamer *Daniel J. Morrell,* examined by Coast Guard Lt. Glen Larsen, marine inspection officer, was later subjected to metallurgical tests.

Plain Dealer *photo*
by William G. Vorpe

One of the last photographs taken of the *Edmund Fitzgerald* clearly shows her two radar antennas. The second radar unit was a relatively recent addition to her equipment. But when she needed them, neither was functional.

CURV III, the remotely powered and controlled drone containing television and photographic equipment, was the vehicle used to document photographically the wreck of the *Edmund Fitzgerald,* 530 feet beneath the surface of Lake Superior.

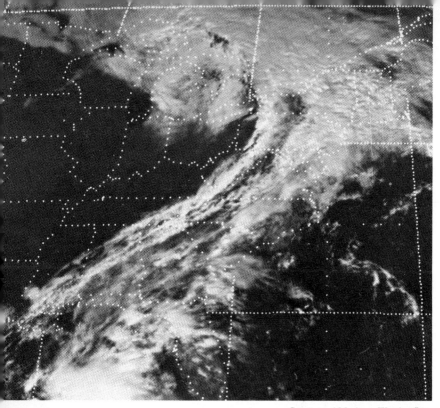

Courtesy of Mariners Weather Log,
National Oceanic and Atmospheric Administration

Satellite image of the storm raging on Lake Superior the night the *Edmund Fitzgerald* disappeared.

Upside-down lettering on the inverted stern section of the *Fitzgerald* quickly identified the wreck.

U.S. Coast Guard photo

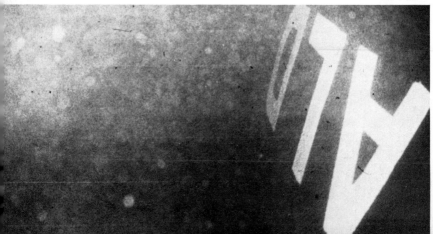

U.S. Coast Guard photo

Under extreme stress, the heavy bottom plates of the *Fitzgerald* simply parted, popping rivets and bending where the stern portion of the wreck separated and turned upside down.

Graphic evidence of the terrible forces of nature are shown in this underwater photo of the torn, twisted, and convoluted one-inch plates of the *Fitzgerald* at one area where the stern separated from the midbody.

U.S. Coast Guard photo

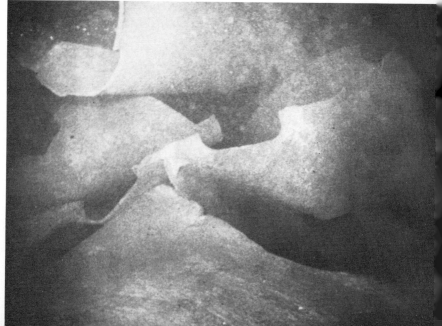

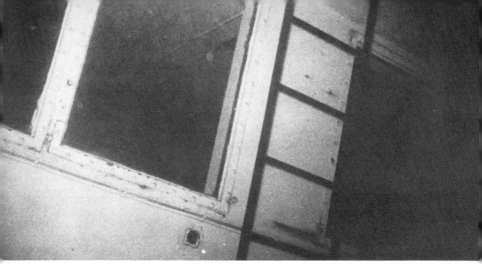

U.S. Coast Guard photo

Rear side of pilot house showing ladder for access to topside equipment. Glass was missing from all windows, either from outside pressure or blown out by compression of air when the structure suddenly filled with water.

Straps from buoyant life jackets hang from the overhead of the pilot house. Note damaged area below and the gyro compass repeater, lower right, outside center window of pilot house.

U.S. Coast Guard photo

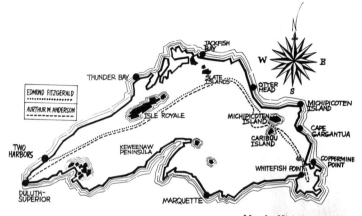

Map by Nickolas Dankovich

Courses steered by the *Arthur M. Anderson* and the *Edmund Fitzgerald* on the fateful night of November 10, 1975.

the Canadian Rescue Coordination Center at Trenton, Ontario, was requested to assist.

All through the balance of that wretched night, fixed-wing aircraft and helicopters criss-crossed the area in designated patterns. Suspicious sightings were marked by flare drops, and the searching steamers battled the seas to check them out. None were productive of any clues or wreckage.

At daylight, Captain Neil Rolfson of the downbound *Roger Blough* reported a significant oil slick, originating about where Captain Cooper had reported the last known position of the *Fitz*.

Later, the surface search force was augmented by the Coast Guard cutter *Woodrush*, out of Duluth. The *Woodrush* had been on six-hour standby duty but had somehow managed to recall all but one man and had departed

Duluth within an hour and a half of the alert. Surface craft combed the area thoroughly for three days with a net harvest of but one of the *Fitz*'s lifeboats, half of another, two self-inflating life rafts, twenty cork life jackets, and miscellaneous flotsam. They found not a single body.

Weekly flights over the area were continued through the end of the year.

In many places around the lakes, where sons, fathers, and husbands had only months before shipped out, there was agonized grieving for the lost crew of the *Fitz*. Lake city churches held special masses and wreaths of sorrow were cast upon the waters.

On November 17th, many survivors of the victims gathered at Toledo's Bay View Armory for memorial services. As the Reverend Robert Armstrong, chaplain of the Port of Toledo, slowly read the names of each of the twenty-nine crewmen, the mellow tone of a brass bell from the former warship USS *Toledo* rang out. A trumpeter played taps as a huge floral wreath was placed aboard a boat that took it out into Lake Erie, there to wander, perhaps forever, on the freshwater seas.

Four hundred and fifty attended, most of them sons, fathers, daughters, wives, and mothers, each with individual burdens of sorrow—sorrow tempered by a great common loss and a thousand prayers for the twenty-nine men lying in the wreck of the *Fitz*, somewhere off Coppermine Point.

But a staunch modern vessel and her crew of twenty-nine do not disappear without generating many questions, doubts, and theories. Some are immediately raised in numbed minds and hearts of those left behind in homes now without fathers and sons. Others come from reasoning men who know ships, shipmasters, and many of the perils they face.

When it was learned that Captain McSorley had described the seas as "tremendous, the worst I have ever seen," many were of the opinion that the *Fitz* had just "submarined" into a massive sea and didn't come up. Even Captain Cooper mentioned this as a possibility, conjecturing that it must have happened just after the last conversation with Captain McSorley.

Others concluded that the *Fitz* was "working" so hard that she cracked plates that later, with continued stresses from hogging and sagging, caused her simply to break in two, going down so swiftly that not a single man could escape. Another possibility advanced was that she broached-to or fell off into the trough of the seas and was capsized, presumably because in the troughs she rolled so drastically that her cargo of iron ore pellets shifted. There was also an erroneous story that she was overloaded.

Still others questioned the construction of Great Lakes vessels, particularly the traditional design of cargo holds, which calls for non-watertight or "screen" connecting bulkheads. And there were those who were highly critical of shipmasters who sail when gale warnings are flying and of companies or owners who permit or encourage them to do so. Some mariners were convinced that the *Fitz* had struck an uncharted pinnacle of rock that had gutted her instantly, and backed this conviction by recalling that Superior Shoal, a series of pinnacles that reach to within twenty-one feet of the surface in Lake Superior, lay undiscovered until the 1930s. Most non-sailors found it incomprehensible that vessels such as the *Fitz* did not have some sort of lifesaving gear that would miraculously enable her people safely to abandon ship.[2]

Official inquiries move slowly but with infinite thoroughness and attention to detail. On the day after the Toledo memorial service, a four-man Coast Guard Marine Board of Investigation met in Cleveland to probe into and determine the circumstances surrounding the loss of the *Fitz* and a possible cause or causes for her foundering.

Headed by Rear Admiral Winford W. Barrow, the board also included Captain James A. Wilson, Commander Charles S. Loosmore, and Captain Adam S. Zabinski, all experts in some phase of marine safety.

Marine Boards of Investigation have the power to administer oaths, summon witnesses, require persons with knowledge of the subject to answer questionnaires, and to demand the production of relevant papers, books, documents, and other evidence.

For eleven days the board painstakingly sought clues to the sudden disappearance of the *Fitz*, interviewing and questioning Coast Guard inspection officers and former skippers and crewmen. With the single exception of remarks from one former crewman, they had nothing but praise for the *Fitz* and the manner in which she was sailed and maintained.

Questions were also put to Weather Bureau experts and the hull supervisor, marine superintendent, and fleet engineer of the Columbia fleet. Also testifying were pilots

---

2 Since the *Daniel J. Morrell* disaster, the Coast Guard has required battery-powered emergency radios in the pilot houses and self-inflating life rafts on all vessels. But the sinking of the *Edmund Fitzgerald* was apparently so precipitous that neither the radio nor life rafts could be utilized.

and masters of vessels in the vicinity of the missing steamer on that mad night of November 10, 1975.

Coast Guard Ensign James J. Gordon inspected the hull on February 19, 1975, and Lt. Chester Walter inspected the lifesaving gear on March 19. Neither noted any deficiencies. Richard A. Feldtz, hull supervisor for Columbia, inspected the *Fitz* only eleven days before she sank and on fourteen previous occasions in 1975, the last time in company with Coast Guard Lt. William Paul and Wilford Jeanquart, American Bureau of Shipping surveyor. Minor irregularities were discovered in the deck area but of such little consequence that the operators were given until April of 1976 to correct them.

Among others, the board heard from Captain Peter Pulcer, previous skipper of the *Fitz*; Captain Albert Jacovetti, pilot of the *Nanfri*; Captain Cooper and first mate Morgan Clark of the *Anderson*; and the pilot of the *Benfri*, Captain Robert O'Brien.

Captain Edgar Jacobsen, marine superintendent for the operators of the *Fitz*, testified that he could not imagine the broken vents reported during the storm permitting enough ingress of water to affect seriously the stability of the vessel, to give her the list Captain McSorley had mentioned.

"As few as one pump, and the ship had four, should be able to take care of that amount of water," he said. He also termed Captain McSorley "our top skipper."

Captain Robert O'Brien, pilot of the *Benfri*, testified that when ships in the area were requested to alter their courses to search for the *Fitz*, the captain of the *Benfri* had refused. In his case, in the tumultuous seas off Coppermine

Point, it would have required coming about. And with two big cranes high on his vessel's deck, the skipper was concerned about capsizing should he fall off into the troughs of the seas while rounding to. He did, however, alter his course thirty degrees, on the possibility of sighting wreckage.

Captain Cedric Woodard, the pilot of the *Avorfors*, the man who had not recognized the voice of his friend, Captain McSorley, was among the last persons to talk to the *Fitz*'s skipper, perhaps the last. "He asked any vessel near Whitefish Point to tell him if its light and radio beacon were functioning," recalled Woodard. "I told him there was no light, but between snow squalls, I could see the tower. And the radio beacon was not operating . . . or at least we couldn't get it. He said he was taking on some water and had developed a list. He gave the impression that he was not in much difficulty, but he sounded worried. I didn't recognize his voice. It didn't sound like him at all."

Captain Charles A. Millradt, commander of the Coast Guard group headquartered at the Soo, told the board that the navigational aids under his command at Whitefish Point had given the Coast Guard problems since automatic equipment had been installed two years previously, replacing a manned station. He stated that there had been a power failure at Whitefish Point on November 10th, the day the *Fitz* was seeking bearings, and that the automatic equipment should have shifted to other power sources but didn't because electronic relays had failed.

When questioned about the cutter *Naugatuck*, stationed at the Soo, being unavailable because of mechanical problems, Captain Millradt admitted that even had the cutter been operational, it could not have gone into the lake in the storm because it was rated unsafe in high winds.[3]

Richard Orgel, who was third mate on the *Fitz* for a month in 1972, reported in a newspaper interview that in even moderately bad weather the 729-foot vessel would bend and spring "like a diving board just after someone dived off it."

However, Andrew Rajner, who was first mate from September 12 to October 3, 1975, as relief for the regular first mate, Jack McCarthy, testified that Captain McSorley never expressed any fears or problems with his ship.[4]

"In fact, he said everything was doing fine," Rajner stated.

Other former officers and seamen also testified that Captain McSorley had always praised the *Fitz*'s behavior and stability and that he found her satisfactory in every way.

The springing action mentioned by Orgel, as experienced seamen know, is the natural response of a vessel adjusting to the rise and fall or hogging and sagging as wave support varies along a long hull. *Not* to spring would

[3] When the government allocates funds for the military, the U.S. Coast Guard, traditionally and regrettably, usually enjoys an exceedingly low priority. This has led to economies such as the closing of many Great Lakes lifeboat stations and the automation of many existing and important lighthouses and aids to navigation. Lake sailors have little faith in automated equipment, and the Whitefish Point light and radio beacon is a case in point. When it was needed it wasn't functioning.

[4] Few men were more liked and respected than John H. McCarthy, first mate of the *Edmund Fitzgerald*. A shipmaster in his own right, he was a licensed officer in the Columbia fleet for thirty-two years. A cheerful, bubbling individual, he was also a good and close friend of Captain Ernest McSorley. Both were within a few years of retirement. Jack McCarthy enjoyed the unique distinction of having been twice elected president of Cleveland Lodge No. 4, the International Shipmasters' Association.

indicate deficiency in design, a vessel too "stiff" and possibly subject to stress fractures.

As time went on, some of the fears, theories, and doubts expressed earlier were being allayed or ruled unlikely.

It was shown by dock records that the *Fitz* was not overloaded, but was actually sailing with a cargo somewhat under her rated capacity.

Although there was no proof or eyewitness to verify the point, it was considered unlikely by most marine men that the *Fitz* broke in half due to stress of weather. There were other vessels out on Lake Superior under the same conditions that night, vessels light or in ballast and thus more prone to hull failure. They also noted that had the *Fitz* indeed succumbed to high seas and broken in half, it would have been the first instance of a *loaded* iron-ore carrier surrendering to stress of weather. For example, the *William Clay Ford*, which left the security of Whitefish Bay to search for the *Fitz*, was an older vessel and in ballast. Yet she survived the same seas without damage.

The undetected-pinnacle-of-rock theory also evaporated when the Canadians resurveyed the area after the disaster. Using the very latest in sophisticated position-finding and fathometer gear, they found no significant or undetected projections. The survey did, however, point out that the 1919 survey and chart was remarkable for its accuracy. (The Canadian chart, incidentally, is much more thorough and complete than the United States charts, showing not only North Bank but other areas where shoal waters exist.)

The eleven days of hearing by the board produced over 3000 pages of testimony, all of it pertinent to the life and times of the *Fitz* but none of it really explaining her sudden disappearance.

More evidence was needed, but only the sunken hull of the *Fitz* could provide additional information, and even that possibility was somewhat remote. Still, the effort had to be made.

Four days after the steamer went down a magnetic-anomaly-detection-device-equipped U.S. Navy aircraft, its equipment calibrated on a vessel similar to the *Fitz* and carrying the same cargo, made a series of flights over the general area of the sinking. One significant contact was made. Side-scan sonar gear, owned and operated by the Coast Guard, was brought to the scene to locate and attempt to verify the wreck. This first search was successful in locating what was firmly believed to be the missing vessel. Sonar traces showed that two pieces of shipwreck were there, in something over 500 feet of water.

But winter, brutal on the upper lakes, had already set in. The location was plotted, but further investigation was postponed until May. During late November, however, the U.S. Navy's Supervisor of Salvage, contacted to provide search consultation, had his primary search-and-recovery contractor, Seaward, Inc., conduct a second side-scan sonar search. Operations were subsequently halted by weather conditions.

At this time, the chairman of the investigative board authorized the commander of the Ninth Coast Guard District, Rear Admiral James S. Gracey, to form a task force that would document by underwater photography and television, the location and condition of the wreck.

Services and resources included side-scan sonar from Seaward, Inc., for relocating of the wreck and setting a moor over the site, and a deep-diving, tethered, submersible CURV III vehicle from the Navy Undersea Center in San Diego, which would be used to obtain photographic and television documentation. (CURV stands for Cable-Controlled Underwater Recovery Vehicle.)

The CURV III system is composed of an underwater vehicle, cable, and surface control equipment. It is capable of working at depths of 7000 feet and is very similar to the device that recovered a lost hydrogen bomb from the coastal waters off Spain in 1966. The cable and surface control and recording systems enable the vehicle to be deployed and remotely operated from a support ship, in this case the Coast Guard cutter *Woodrush*.

In the eight days following the positioning of the *Woodrush* over the site, CURV III made twelve dives, logging fifty-six hours and forty minutes of bottom time, recording over 43,000 feet of video tape, and snapping almost 900 35mm color slides.

It was a first for this type of operation for the Coast Guard on the Great Lakes. Ironically, the wreckage straddles the waters of the international boundary line between the United States and Canada.

Strangely, too, the earlier sonar traces had indicated the wreckage to be in two, three, or possibly four pieces, but upright. But the video pictures, as proven by finding the vessel's name and home port clearly visible, showed that the stern of the *Fitz* was upside down.

Recorded observation on film and videotape show that the stern section separated at approximately frame 178 and is upside down on the after superstructure. The rudder, the propeller, and exposed bottom appear to be undamaged.

The close proximity of all the wreckage seemed to indicate to marine people further proof that the *Fitz* did not suffer a sudden and clean break due to stress of weather. They point out the only recent documented evidence of such an incident occurred in 1966, when the *Daniel J. Morrell*, under weather conditions similar to those experienced by the *Fitz*, broke in half suddenly and completely in Lake Huron. The lone survivor, Dennis Hale, recounted how the stern half, still under power, pushed the forward end aside and continued on up the lake, lights bright, and the propeller still thrashing full ahead. Had the *Fitz* fractured so abruptly, they reasoned, the after end would have continued to charge on for at least a short period of time. In any event, it would not be where it was.

The bow section of the *Fitz* is sitting nearly upright, buried to her twenty-seven-foot mark in mud, separated at about frame Seventy-five and between hatches Eight and Nine. The starboard side of the hull at the separation point is bent in and folds under the deck. The bow superstructure is intact, but damaged. A combination of mud and taconite pellets is spread and stacked over all deck spaces. The main deck and its equipment, including hatch coamings, are badly damaged. Extending outward from the separations at the stern and bow sections are extensive areas of debris, which, for the most part, appear to be from the interior of the vessel, awe-inspiring evidence of massive, destructive forces. At the stern section, it is probable that this debris extends upward through the bottom mud from a portion of the deck still attached to the stern.

It all remains there without really saying very much or revealing anything that could lead to *positive* conclusions.

Captain James S. Wilson, a member of the Coast Guard Marine Board of Investigation, summed it up by saying that the 729-foot *Fitzgerald*, if stood on end, would stick 209 feet above Lake Superior's surface. "But on the bottom," he observed, "she might as well be on the moon for all we can find out!"

Finding the *Fitz*'s propeller and rudder undamaged and her stern area relatively intact and probably still operational at the time of the disaster, led some to wonder if the ship, with her more than 26,000 tons of cargo would have plowed into the bottom with the propeller still pushing as she submerged, bow-first. Theoretically, this could account for the "telescoping" collapse and severe structural damage and distortion of the midships area.

During the interim period between the sinking and the final underwater survey, however, there came a growing conviction in the minds of the board and marine men of long experience that what sent the *Fitz* down for the count was not what happened between 7:10 P.M. and 7:15 P.M. that terrible night in the storm, snow, and darkness, but what happened between 3:00 and 3:30 that afternoon, north of Caribou.

They conclude, almost unanimously now, that the *Fitz* did indeed touch bottom, perhaps twice, on the North Bank shoal off Caribou, but that in the stress of weather, with the *Fitz* pounding heavily in monster seas, the shock was not detected by Captain McSorley or any of the crew. But contact with the hard rock shoal might have done enough damage seriously to affect the vessel's hull or "girder" strength. Subsequently then, they surmise, the damage proliferated in the form of fracturing, shearing, or tearing plates, frames, and even the lower ballast tank tops as the *Fitz* hogged, sagged, and twisted in incredibly severe seas over a period of three and one-half hours.

And again, without her master or crew being aware of impending disaster, the end would have come without warning, without time to don life jackets or rush to the inflatable life rafts. The time required to lower lifeboats would have rendered them useless.

This would account for the list Captain McSorley reported, shortly after passing near or over the shoal area. Captain Jacobsen and others had previously doubted whether the broken ballast tank vents could have permitted the ingress of enough water to give the *Fitz* a list. In any event, the ship had pumps to handle that amount of water easily. No, without a doubt, something else had transpired to give the vessel a noticeable list.

And the evidence that could not be discounted was the testimony of Captain Cooper, who, before the board and obviously reluctant to question the judgment of a fellow skipper, said that the *Fitz* was, in the estimation of himself and First Mate Morgan Clark, "close, too close." And in a telephone conversation with his superiors, Captain Cooper had been even more specific. "I mean, God, he was about three miles off the beacon."

Vice-Admiral (Ret.) Paul E. Trimble, president of the

Lake Carriers' Association, agreed. In a letter to Melvin Pelfrey, vice-president of the Marine Engineers Beneficial Association, he said that data gathered by the Canadian government during a sounding survey of the six-fathom shoal area off Caribou Island makes it "very likely" that the vessel "bottomed in the sea conditions that existed and started the chain of events which led to her eventually breaking in two."

Admiral Winslow W. Barrow, Chairman of the Coast Guard Marine Board of Investigation was also convinced that the *Fitz* "touched" on the lurking rock shoal. "Something happened to the *Fitzgerald* between 3:00 P.M. and 3:30 P.M. north of Caribou Island," he reflected.

"At that time, the ship started taking on water and taking a list, and her master reported that, by radio. And, subsequently, the hull suffered a rather sudden failure. That happened after dark on November 10, some three hours down the lake from where the first report came, an hour away from shelter at Whitefish Point.

"And I can imagine," Admiral Barrow said, "that there was some damage when she hit bottom. If I had my choice of things to know, though, it would be what happened at 3:00 P.M. or 3:15 P.M., because the other things flowed from that."

Unfortunately, not admirals, shipbuilders, naval architects, nor sailors are blessed with the psychic gift of wringing documented evidence from inanimate and soulless wreckage lying 530 feet deep in cold and dark Lake Superior. At best, there is only studied, knowledgeable conjecture—but conjecture based on vast experience blended with evidence yielded in the hearing room and those photographs from the murky depths of the lake the Chippewas used to call Gitche Gumee, the Shining Big-Sea-Water.[5] As long as ships sail the Great Lakes and there are men to sail them, there will undoubtedly be an element of doubt, conflicting theories, and the mindless questioning of men who never went down to the seas in ships.[6]

On dark and windy nights, as long as steamers pass over the grave of the *Fitz*, there will always be the inevitable quiet pilot house thesis: "They say she hit a shoal, did damage to her bottom, and later broke in two. But then . . ."

The *Fitz* is gone, the last wreath cast upon the waters, the last bell tolled for her twenty-nine men. But for those they left behind, the tears will never cease.

[5] Marine Boards of Investigation are not made up of harsh, vindictive individuals, but of knowledgeable, understanding men capable of compassion, but firm in upholding the highest standards of seamanship, navigation, and marine safety.

In the case of the *Fitz*, board members were aware of all the potential or possible causes for the loss. But, in the absence of eyewitnesses, they were also cognizant that all the evidence presented was circumstantial. They were also conscious that Captain McSorley, deprived of both radars and the Caribou Island and Whitefish Point radio beacons, could, because of snow and poor visibility, have been off his course or even lost. They knew that, unlike Marine Boards of Investigation, he did not have weeks or months to reach a decision, only moments.

[6] During the spring and summer after the *Fitz* disappeared, both Americans and Canadians heard an account of the shipwreck as related in the haunting ballad "The Wreck of the *Edmund Fitzgerald*," composed by Canadian folk singer Gordon Lightfoot. Starting slowly, the song climbed steadily to the top in ratings. Its somber but thrilling message aroused much interest in the Great Lakes, especially among young listeners. People who never before had expressed an interest in the lakes were suddenly conscious of their importance and of the dangers inherent in sailing them.

Bibliography

Ashtabula, Ohio. *Star-Beacon*. December 1, 2, 1966.

———. November 12, 1975.

Benton Harbor, Michigan. *News-Palladium*, December 4, 1908.

Bliss, Philip P. *Memoirs of Philip P. Bliss*. Barnes, A. S. & Co., 1878.

Brinks, Dr. Herbert J. "The Era of Pig Iron in the Upper Peninsula of Michigan." *Inland Seas*. Fall 1969.

Buffalo, New York. *Commercial*. August 10, 1851.

Buffalo, New York. *Courier Express*. December 1, 1966.

Chicago, Illinois. *Tribune*. December 5, 1908.

Cleveland, Ohio. *Leader*. July 1, 1899.

Cleveland, Ohio. *Plain Dealer*. November 29, 30, 1966.

———. December 1, 3, 6, 9, 12, 17, 22, 24, 1966.

———. January 1, 4, 7, 12, 24, 1967.

———. November 11, 12, 13, 19, 20, 21, 22, 23, 24, 25, 27, 29, 1975.

———. December 12, 14, 15, 1975.

———. May 21, 1976.

———. August 21, 1976.

Cleveland, Ohio. *Press*. November 29, 1966.

———. December 1, 7, 11, 20, 1966.

———. November 11, 12, 17, 19, 21, 25, 28, 1975.

Detroit Marine Historian. Vol. 15. May 1962.

Detroit, Michigan. *Free Press.* December 1, 2, 3, 4, 1966.

———. November 11, 18, 1975.

———. May 22, 1976.

Detroit, Michigan. *News.* November 30, 1966.

———. December 1, 1966.

———. November 12, 1975.

Erie, Pennsylvania. *Gazette.* August 12, 1851.

Erie, Pennsylvania. *Observer.* August 12, 1851.

Ferguson, Jeremy. "On the Waterfront." *Key to Toronto.*

Frimodig, Mac. *Shipwrecks off the Keweenaw.* Fort Wilkins Natural History Association in cooperation with the Michigan Department of Natural Resources.

The Great Lakes Historical Society. *Inland Seas.* Summer 1959, Winter 1967, Spring 1968.

Great Lakes Maritime Institute. *Telescope.* March-April 1972.

Havighurst, Walter. *Vein of Iron.* Cleveland, Ohio: World Publishing Co., 1958.

———. *The Long Ships Passing.* New York: The Macmillan Co., 1945.

Hawkins, Larry. "*A Night to Remember.*" Cleveland, Ohio. *Plain Dealer.* December 30, 1956.

Houghton, Michigan. *Daily Mining Gazette.* November 13, 1971.

———. November 24, 1974.

Lake Carriers' Association. *Bulletin.* August-September 1969.

Kelly, S. J. "Memories of Historic Cleveland." Cleveland, Ohio. *Plain Dealer.* August 3, 1935.

Mansfield, J. B. *History of the Great Lakes.* Chicago: J. H. Beer & Co., 1899.

Marquette, Michigan. *Mining Journal.* November 20, 27, 1869.

———. December 4, 11, 25, 1869.

———. January 1, 9, 1870.

———. April 23, 30, 1870.

———. May 7, 1870.

Milwaukee, Wisconsin. *Sentinel.* December 5, 1908.

National Oceanic and Atmospheric Administration. *Mariners Weather Log.* Washington, D.C. May 1976.

National Transportation Board, U.S. Coast Guard Marine Board of Investigation, *Daniel J. Morrell,* 1967.

Ogdensburg, New York. *St. Lawrence Republican.* December 9, 1908.

Painesville, Ohio. *Telegraph.* November 30, 1966.
———. November 11, 12, 20, 22, 28, 1975.
———. December 1, 12, 1975.
Port Huron, Michigan. *Times-Herald.* December 1, 2, 3, 1966.
———. September 15, 1968.
Sturgeon Bay, Wisconsin. *Door County Advocate.* October 5, 1903.
Toledo, Ohio. *Blade.* November 11, 18, 1975.
Willoughby, Ohio. *News-Herald.* November 11, 15, 17, 20, 24, 1975.
———. December 1, 12, 13, 1975.

Index

199